PLAYFUL
TRADITIONS

Playful Traditions

A Jewish Preschool Book of Holiday Games and Ideas

Marcia Shemaria Green

Humanics Learning
Atlanta, GA USA

HUMANICS LEARNING

Playful Traditions
A Humanics Learning Publication

Humanics Learning Publications are an imprint of and published by Humanics Publishing Group, a division of Brumby Holdings, LLC. It's trademark, consisting of the words "Humanics Learning" and a portrayal of a silhouetted girl, is registered in the U.S. Patent Office and in other countries.

Brumby Holdings, LLC
1197 Peachtree Street
Suite 533 Plaza
Atlanta, GA 30361

Printed in the United States of America

Library of Congress Control Number: 2001091311
ISBN (Paperback): 0-89334-344-7
ISBN (Hardcover): 0-89334-345-5

Table of Contents

Introduction

These games and ideas offer an easy, relaxed way for children to explore the Holidays and have fun in the process. Most of the games presented here are for nonreaders and should first be introduced by the teacher to the children. There are interactive and individual games; card games and matching picture games; games for 2-4 players and games for one player. On some of the games, Hebrew and its transliteration have been provided along with the English word for the picture. And because some of the Hebrew is Yiddish and pronounced differently than the given English word, an additional meaning of the Hebrew is given in ( ) under the transliteration.

For example: Hamanatashen, אָזְנֵי הָמָן, oz-nei Ham-man, translates to (Haman's ears). Please note: Hebrew is read from right to left.

All the pictures necessary to create the game boards are provided. The (*) indicates pictures included in this book. Other materials are easily available: file folders, colored markers or pencils, glue, scissors, tape, manila and business sized envelopes, paper, Velcro, hole punch, zippered pencil pouches, etc.

A pencil pouch or an envelope can be used to store the game pieces for the file folder games. Use Velcro to attach the pencil pouch or envelope to the back of the folder. Velcro can be used to keep the envelope flap closed.

Tag board or cardboard make sturdy backings for many of the game pieces. Laminating everything will allow the games to last longer.

In order to preserve the originals, trace or photocopy the patterns to create the games. If a piece is lost, the original is available to create a replacement.

Saving discarded game boards, with spinners, dice and movers, will increase your ability to enhance some of the games. Cover discarded game boards with white paper, then add the necessary pictures to create the designated game. When the game board is complete, cover with clear contact paper. Buttons or colored marker tops may be used for movers.

Have fun and enjoy watching your students learn while playing!

Marcia Shemaria Green

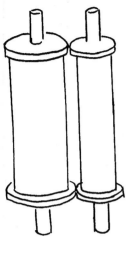

SHABBAT

Background Information for Shabbat

WORDS TO KNOW:

Belt (Binder): A long band of material, usually 2 to 3 inches wide, used to encircle the two rolls of the Torah and hold them together.

Breast Plate (Shield): Generally made of silver and measures about 8 to 10 inches attached to a chain and draped over the two poles of the Torah.

Candles: At least two candles are lit on Shabbat to represent the two important references to the Sabbath in the Bible: "Remember the Sabbath" and "Observe the Sabbath."

Challahs: Two braided breads eaten on Shabbat. The two challahs remind us that when the Israelites were in the wilderness on their way to the Promised Land, on Fridays they collected a double portion of manna (food that fell from the sky), because on Saturday(Shabbat) they were not allowed to collect food.

Cover (Mantle): The Torah is too precious to leave uncovered. Therefore, a garment of velvet or silk is used to cover, protect and beautify the Torah. During the High Holidays the Torah is covered with a white Mantle.

Crown: The Torah is the holiest object in Jewish life and therefore it is natural to crown it with a symbol of kingship.

Kiddush Cup: Wine cup used to hold the wine on Shabbat.

Noah: A good and righteous man whom the Lord spoke to telling him to build an Ark for his family and 2 of each animal as the Lord was going to flood the Earth.

Noah's Ark: Refers to the vessel the Lord specifically told Noah to build that sheltered Noah, his family, and all the animals during the great flood.

Shabbat: A Jewish Sabbath, a day of rest.

Torah: The first five books of the Bible, written on a parchment scroll, rolled on two wooden pins, and is read in synagogue. The Torah scrolls are kept in a special cabinet known as the Holy Ark. The Torah is hand written by a scribe (a devout scholar and calligrapher) without punctuation and vowel markings, using a special quill and ink.

Yad: Means "hand" in Hebrew. It is a silver stick with a hand or finger at one end. The "Yad" helps the reader keep their place as well as protects the ink from smudging.

BACKGROUND:

Shabbat is observed every week throughout the year. Shabbat begins on Friday night at sunset and ends on Saturday night at sunset. When Shabbat begins two candles are lit and prayers are said over them, a cup of wine, and two challah breads. Shabbat is a day of rest as stated in the Bible, where God created the world in six days and rested on the seventh day.

Game: Dress the Torah

(Sequencing, Counting 1-6, Name of Torah Parts in English and Hebrew)

A GAME FOR SHABBAT OR SIMCHAT TORAH

MATERIALS:

6 Torah pieces*(pp. 7-9)	Thin string	Velcro
Dress the Torah "die" pattern*(p. 10)		Tag board
Large manila envelope	Hole punch	Needle

INSTRUCTIONS:

1. Copy the 6 Torah pieces four times onto tag board.

2. Color and cut out the pieces. The words may be glued to the back of each piece in order to identify each piece in Hebrew and English. Laminate all the pieces.

3. Attach a small piece of Velcro to the back of the Belts and the center of each Torah. The Belt will appear to hold the Torah closed. (The ‫ב‬ is at the top of the Torah.)

4. Use the hole punch to cut out the holes of the Mantles.

5. Put a small hole in the Yads using a needle and attach a 6" piece of string to each.

6. Cut the laminate away inside the Breast Plate's "chain" so it will hang over the poles of the Torah.

7. Cut a slit in the Crowns (along the dotted line) so each Crown fits over the poles of the Torah.

8. Copy the "die" pattern onto tag board. Cut out along the dotted lines and laminate. Put the "die" together by folding along the solid lines and taping the edges closed.

9. Design a cover for the envelope and glue the directions and key to the back.

DIRECTIONS TO PLAY DRESS THE TORAH GAME
(1-4 PLAYERS)

1. Place the Torah pieces in the center of the table, giving each piece it's own pile.

2. Decide who will go first. The first player rolls the "die". Whatever picture appears on the top of the "die" the player selects that piece and places it in front of themselves.

3. The next player rolls the "die" and selects the piece displayed.

4. If a player rolls a piece they already have, they do nothing and the play continues to the next player.

5. Play continues until a player has collected all 6 Torah pieces.

6. Now dress the Torah. Keeping the ב at the top of the Torah, attach the Belt to the Torah by the Velcro. Place the Mantle over the poles of the Torah. Hang the Breast Plate by the "chain" over the Torah, on top of the Mantle. Hang the Yad by the string over one pole. Place the Crown on top of the Torah, sliding the poles through the slit.

7. When the Torah has been successfully dressed, the player can say, "Shabbat Shalom." If playing the game for Simchat Torah, the player can say, "Happy Simchat Torah," or another appropriate phase.

VARIATION: For older children, the Torah pieces can be collected sequentially, (1-6), and thus the Torah can be dressed properly as the game goes along.

Dress the Torah Pieces

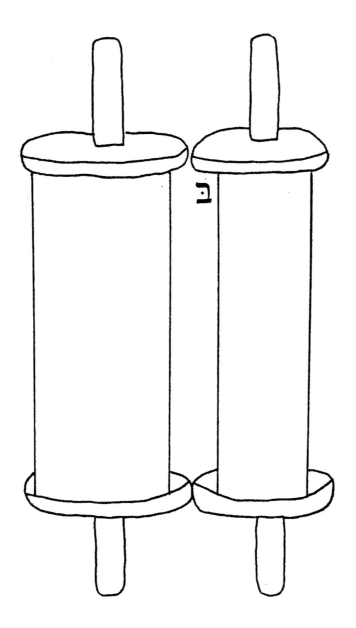

Torah

תּוֹרָה

to-<u>ra</u>

Dress the Torah Pieces

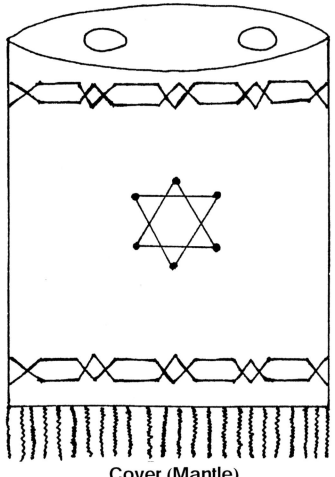

Cover (Mantle)

מְעִיל

me-il

Pointer (Yad)

יָד

yad

Belt (Binder)

חֲגוֹרָה

cha-go-ra

Dress the Torah Pieces

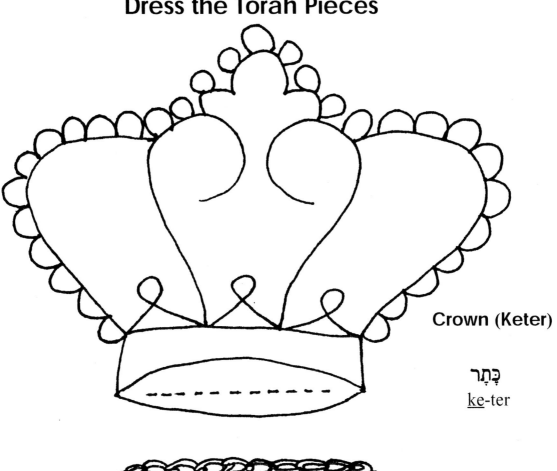

Crown (Keter)

כֶּתֶר
<u>ke</u>-ter

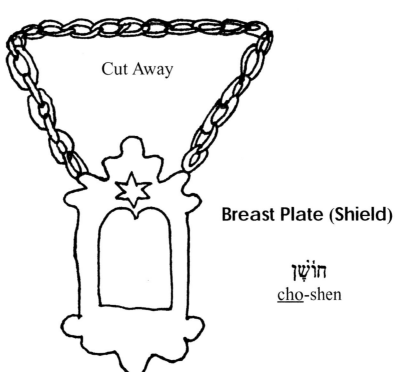

Cut Away

Breast Plate (Shield)

חוֹשֶׁן
<u>cho</u>-shen

Dress the Torah "Die" Pattern

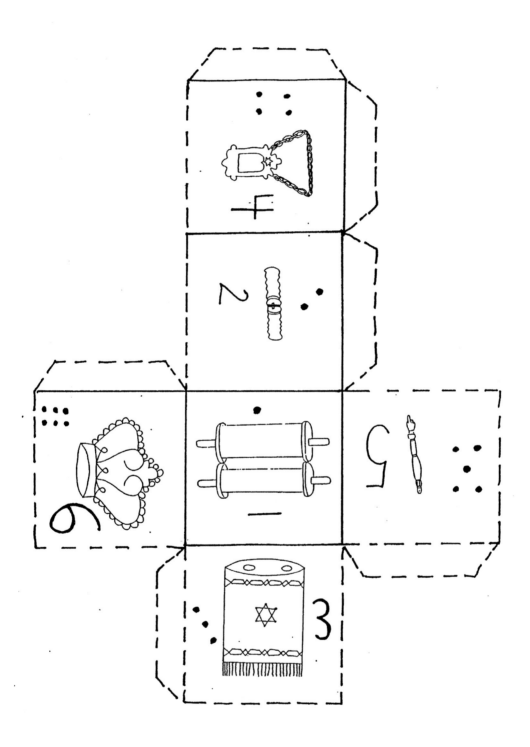

Dress the Torah Key

Key:

1. Torah=

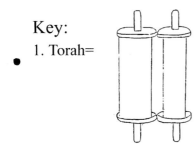

2. Belt (Binder)=

2. Cover (Mantle)=

4. Breast Plate (Shield)=

5. Pointer (Yad)=

6. Crown (Keter)=

Game: Same/Different Game
(Visual Discrimination)

FOR ANY HOLIDAY

MATERIALS:

File folder   Pictures from this book*

Pencil pouch   3"x 5" cards (at least 10, or as many as you wish)

INSTRUCTIONS:

1. Using the inside of a file folder, write the word "**SAME**" on the left side of the folder. Place two identical pictures under the word "**SAME**" and glue down, see page 13.

2. On the right side of the folder, write the word "**DIFFERENT**." Place two different pictures under the word "**DIFFERENT**" and glue down, see page 13.

3. Use the pictures included in this book to design same and different cards. Create "**SAME**" cards by putting 2 identical pictures side by side on a 3" x 5" card. Create "**DIFFERENT**" cards by putting two different pictures side by side on a 3" x 5" card.

4. Design a cover and glue the directions to the back of the file folder.

5. Laminate all the cards and the file folder. Attach a pencil pouch to the back of the folder to store all the cards.

DIRECTIONS TO PLAY SAME/DIFFERENT GAME
(ONE PLAYER)

1. The player removes all the cards from the pencil pouch.

2. By looking at the pictures, the player will identify each card as having "**SAME**" or "**DIFFERENT**" pictures and place the card on the appropriate side of the folder.

EXAMPLE:

EXTRA CHALLENGE: The player could identify what holiday the pictures represent.

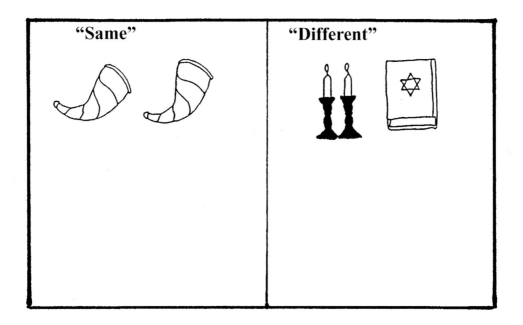

Game: Noah's Ark
(Matching Pairs, Names of Animals in English and Hebrew)

MATERIALS:

Ark pattern* (p. 17)   Animal patterns* (pp. 15-16)
Tag board   Large Manila envelope

INSTRUCTIONS:

1. Enlarge and copy the picture of the Ark four times onto tag board. Color the Arks four different shades of brown.

2. Make two copies of the animals. Color each animal pair the same color. Remember to color the Raven black and the Dove white. Mount the animals on tag board and cut out the squares.

3. Laminate the Arks and animal squares.

4. Design a cover on a large envelope and glue the directions to the back. Keep the game pieces in the envelope.

DIRECTIONS TO PLAY NOAH'S ARK GAME
(2-4 PLAYERS)

1. Players select their own Ark.

2. Place the animal cards face down in the center of the table.*

3. Decide who will go first. The first player turns over two cards. If the animals match, the player puts the pair on the Ark. If the animals do not match, the cards are turned back and the next player goes.

4. Play continues until all the animals are matched and placed on an Ark.

*NOTE TO TEACHER: Based on the children's ages and ability, select the number of animal pairs for your students to work with in order to avoid frustration or boredom. Remember to include the Raven and the Dove in this number.

Noah's Ark Animal Patterns

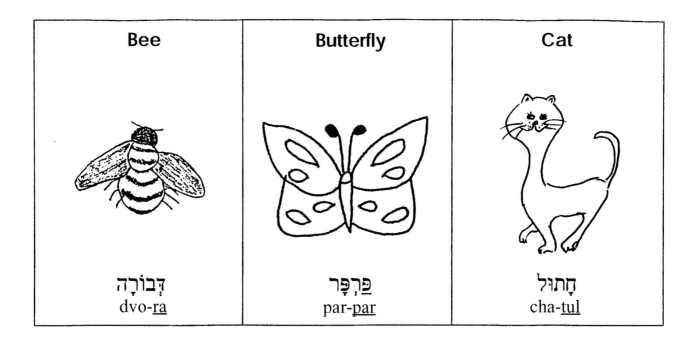

Bee	Butterfly	Cat
דְּבוֹרָה	פַּרְפַּר	חָתוּל
dvo-<u>ra</u>	par-<u>par</u>	cha-<u>tul</u>

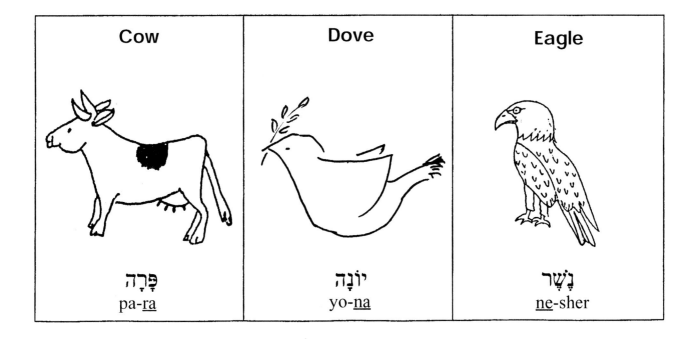

Cow	Dove	Eagle
פָּרָה	יוֹנָה	נֶשֶׁר
pa-<u>ra</u>	yo-<u>na</u>	<u>ne</u>-sher

Noah's Ark Animal Patterns

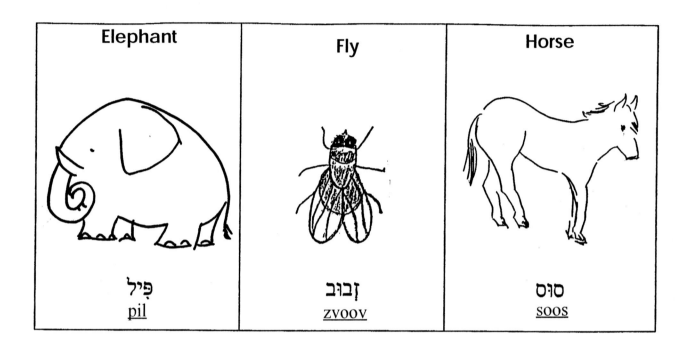

Elephant

פִּיל
pil

Fly

זְבוּב
zvoov

Horse

סוּס
soos

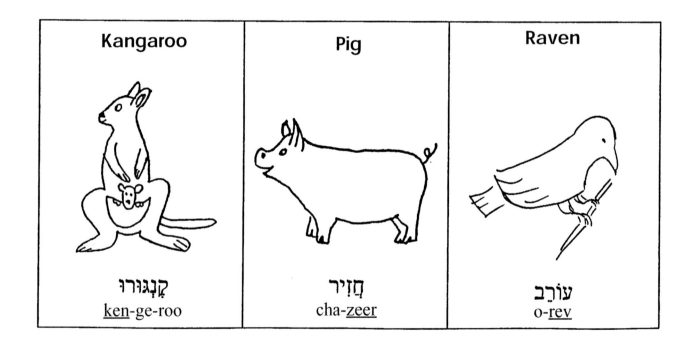

Kangaroo

קֶנְגּוּרוּ
ken-ge-roo

Pig

חֲזִיר
cha-zeer

Raven

עוֹרֵב
o-rev

Noah's Ark Pattern

תֵּבַת־נֹחַ
tei-vat no-ach

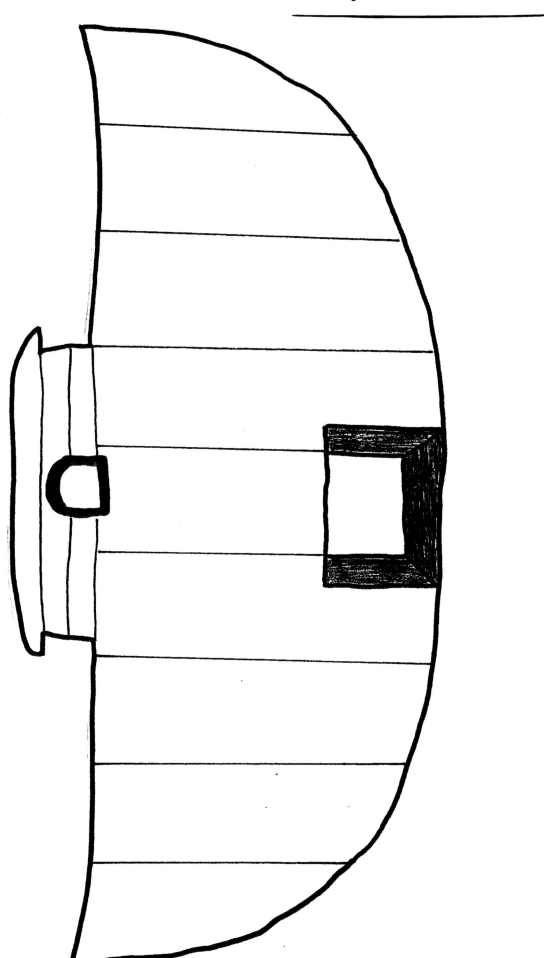

Art: Ark Art Idea

MATERIALS:

Ark pattern* (p. 17)   Animal stamps or stickers (not provided)

INSTRUCTIONS:

1. Copy enough Ark patterns, one for each child.

2. Have the children color their Arks.

3. Using animal stamps or stickers, the children put two of each animal on their Ark.

4. Other details such as Noah, water, the mountains of Ararat, and a rainbow can be added to their creations.

The Story of Noah and the Ark

Once a long time ago, God became disappointed with the people on Earth. All except for Noah, who was a good and righteous man. So God said to Noah, "I am going to flood the Earth. Make an Ark with compartments, three floors, a door on the side and a window. Take your three sons: Shem, Ham and Japheth; your wife, and your son's wives and two of each animal - a male and a female. Take food and store it away for your family and the animals. Take everything into the Ark."

When Noah was 600 years old, in the second month, on the 17th day of the month, the rain fell on the Earth 40 days and 40 nights.

At the end of 150 days, the water diminished so that in the seventh month on the 17th day of the month, the Ark came to rest on the mountains of Ararat.

In the tenth month on the first of the month, the tops of the mountains became visible.

At the end of 40 days, Noah opened the window of the Ark and sent out a raven but it didn't return. Then Noah sent out a dove and the dove came back because there was still water over the Earth and the dove couldn't find a place to land. A week later, Noah sent the dove out again. This time the dove returned with an olive leaf in its bill! Then Noah knew the waters had decreased on the Earth.

In the six hundred and first year, in the first month on the first of the month, the waters began to dry from the Earth. When Noah opened the door, he saw that the surface of the ground was drying. And in the second month on the 27th day of the month, the Earth was dry.

God said to Noah, "Come out of the Ark together with your wife, your sons, and your son's wives. Bring out all the animals and let them go free to increase on the Earth."

The Lord said to Himself, "Never again will I doom the Earth because of man, nor will I ever again destroy every living being as I have done. I will place a bow in the sky as a sign that I promise never to destroy the Earth again."

NOTE: This story of Noah may contain more information than your students need. You may adjust this story to fit the needs of your students.

Art: Shabbat Place Mats
(Use for Snack or Lunch on Fridays)

MATERIALS:
Challah patterns*(p. 21)   Candlestick patterns*(p. 22)   Kiddush cup patterns*(p. 23)
1" x 2" Candles* (2 per child) (p. 22)   Tag board or cardboard

INSTRUCTIONS:
1. Copy the pattern pieces several times onto tag board or cardboard and cut out.

2. Either the child or the teacher can trace each pattern onto the appropriate color of construction paper. (For example: Kiddush cup on purple, Candle sticks on orange, Challahs on brown, leave the candles white.) Cut out each piece.

3. The child selects their own 12" x 18" sheet of colored construction paper for their placemat, and glues the pieces down.

4. Glue the two "candles" onto the candlesticks.

5. The child can then decorate the placemat by adding black dots on the Challahs to represent raisins, color the Kiddush cup purple for wine, or add flames to the candles.

6. The Hebrew and English words can be added to identify each object.

7. Write the child's name and date on the placemat and laminate.

8. The placemats can be used on Fridays for Shabbat snack or lunch at school.

9. Send the placemats home at the end of the year.

*Hebrew provided.

Shabbat Placemat Patterns

Challahs

חַלּוֹת
cha-<u>lot</u>

Shabbat Placemat Patterns

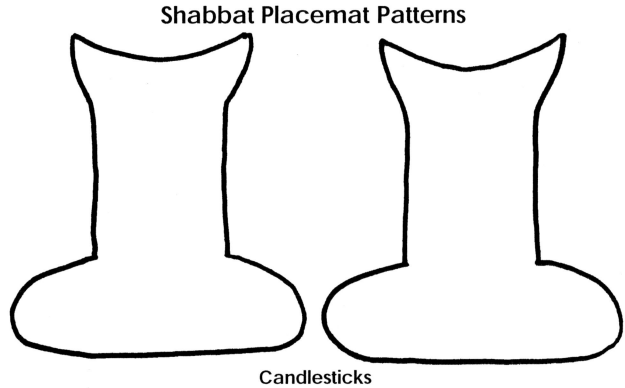

Candlesticks

פַּמוֹטִים

pa-mo-<u>tim</u>

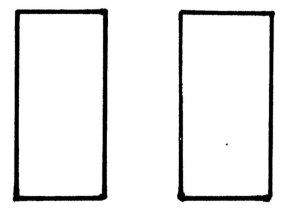

Candles

נֵרוֹת

ne-<u>rot</u>

Shabbat Placemat Patterns

Kiddush Cup

כּוֹס קִדּוּשׁ
kos ki-doosh

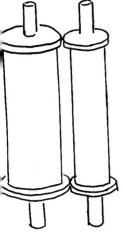

HIGH HOLIDAYS

Background Information for the High Holidays

WORDS TO KNOW:

Apples and Honey: Two foods eaten on Rosh Hashanah for a sweet New Year. The sweet apples are dipped into the sweeter honey.

Eternal Light: A light in the Synagogue above the Holy Ark that is never permitted to go out.

Etrog: A hardy, pale yellow and fragrant fruit resembling a lemon, that can last the seven days of Sukkot. Also called a citron. The Etrog is used along with the Lulav during Sukkot.

Honey: Apple and pieces of challah are dipped in honey with the wish that the coming year might be as sweet as honey.

Jonah: "The Story of Jonah" is read in the afternoon service on Yom Kippur.

Lulav: In Hebrew, "Lulav" means a branch from the date palm tree. It is the plural name for the set of three species: a sheaf of long palm fronds bound with a willow branch and a myrtle branch. The Lulav is used along with the Etrog during Sukkot.

Prayer Book: Contains passages from the Bible. It is mostly written in Hebrew.

Rosh Hoshana: The Jewish New Year that means "the head of the year" in Hebrew and is traditionally regarded as the day of the world's creation. A serious holiday as well as a time of festive joy because people have an opportunity to repent and begin anew.

Round Challahs: For Rosh Hashanah the challahs are round, like the cycle of the year, symbolizing the hope for a full year and a long life.

Shemini Atzeret: The eighth day of Sukkot, also known as the "Eighth Day of Assembly." An extra day the sages added to the end of Sukkot, as a day to pray for rain and in later years, a memorial service for the dead was added.

Shofar: A ram's horn blown several times during Rosh Hashanah services to welcome the New Year and at the end of Yom Kippur.

Simchat Torah: The ninth day of Sukkot, also known as the Rejoicing in the Law. A second day the sages added to Sukkot to honor the Torah.

Sukkah: A temporary three-sided outdoor booth. The roof is covered with vines, tree branches, or other plants so it provides shade in the day and the stars are visible at night. Fruits and/or vegetables, or child made paper decorations are hung from the roof to decorate the Sukkah.

Sukkot: The name of a holiday and the plural of (Sukkah). During the Exodus from Egypt (see the Story of Moses, A Story for Passover) it is the place where the fleeing Israelite slaves stopped for the first time as a free people.

Synagogue: A place of worship, study, and assembly for the Jewish people.

Torah: The first five books of the Bible, written on a parchment scroll, and is read in synagogue.

Yom Kippur: The Day of Atonement and the holiest day of the Jewish year. It is a day of complete fasting in order to seek forgiveness for their sins and reconciliation with God.

BACKGROUND:

The ten-day period known as the High Holy Days start with Rosh Hashanah on the first day of Tishrei, on the Jewish calendar, and end ten days later with Yom Kippur. These are the two most intensely religious days of the Jewish calendar. There is no "story," historical event, or seasonal celebration associated with these two Holidays as there are in other Jewish holidays throughout the year. Rosh Hashanah is the Jewish New Year and in Hebrew means "the head of the year." Rosh Hashanah celebrates the day on which the world was created. Yom Kippur in Hebrew means, "Day of Atonement" and is the holiest day of the Jewish year. Forgiveness for sin is the major theme of Yom Kippur. It is also a day of self-affliction, and a day of complete fasting from sunset on the eve of Yom Kippur to sunset the following day.

Sukkot occurs five days after Yom Kippur ends. Sukkot is a festival holiday that lasts for 7 days (Plus two extra days) beginning on the 15th day of Tishrei. Also called the Festival of Booths or the Harvest Festival.

During Sukkot, people eat as many meals as possible in the Sukkah, unless it is raining. On the eighth day of Sukkot a new festival called Shemini Atzeret, meaning the "Eighth day of Solemn Assembly," is celebrated. A memorial service for the dead and prayers for rain in Israel during this, their dry season, celebrates the Holiday.

And then at last comes Simchat Torah, the Rejoicing in the Law, a holiday dedicated to the Torah. Simchat Torah marks the day we finish reading the last chapter of the Torah and begin again reading the first chapter of Creation. There is a celebration of dancing, singing, and flag waving, as all the Torahs in the synagogue are carefully taken from the Holy Ark and are lovingly carried and paraded around the synagogue.

These are the four Holidays of the month Tishrei.

Game: High Holiday Game
(Matching, 1 to 1 Correspondence,
Naming Holiday Symbols in English and Hebrew)

A GAME FOR ROSH HASHANAH, YOM KIPPUR, SUKKOT, AND SIMCHAT TORAH

MATERIALS:

House pattern*(p. 31)	Synagogue pattern*(p.31)	4 Movers
Discarded gameboard or large file folder		11 Holiday symbols*(pp. 31, 32)
Pencil pouch	Optional: Spinner (p. 30)	

INSTRUCTIONS:

1. Use the discarded gameboard covered with white paper, or a large file folder, to create the gameboard.

2. Copy, color, and cut out the House and Synagogue.

3. Place the House in the lower left corner and the Synagogue in the upper right corner of the gameboard or opened file folder.

4. Make enough copies of the Holiday symbols to form a path from the House to the Synagogue, plus one extra set. Color and cut out the symbols.

5. Vary the Holiday symbols to form a snake-like path from the House to the Synagogue. Place a symbol (like the Eternal Light) on the Synagogue as a final move.

6. Use the extra set of symbols to create a spinner, or keep the cards loose to form a pile. Laminate spinner or cards.

7. Either cover the gameboard with clear contact paper or laminate the file folder.

8. Store game pieces and directions in the pencil pouch attached to the gameboard.

DIRECTIONS TO PLAY HIGH HOLIDAY GAME
(2-4 PLAYERS)

1. Each player selects a mover and places it on the House.

2. Decide who will go first. First player either spins the spinner, or turns over the top card; and moves to the matching symbol, always moving towards the Synagogue. If using the "pile" method, reshuffle the cards each time they are used up.

3. Play continues in this manner to all players.

4. If a symbol is picked, (or landed on by the spinner), that is not in front of the player, the player doesn't move. Play continues to the next player.

5. As each player reaches the Synagogue, they can say, "La Shana Tova!"

HOW TO CREATE A SPINNER

TO CREATE A SPINNER FROM A DISCARDED GAME:

1. Trace the outline of the spinner onto white paper.

2. Make a slit from the edge of the paper, to the center of the paper.

3. Glue the paper to the spinner using the slit to fit around the spinner.

4. To use the spinner with the High Holiday Game, glue the 11 pictures to the edge of the spinner and draw lines to separate each picture.

5. Cover with clear contact paper.

TO MAKE YOUR OWN SPINNER:

1. Buy clock hands from a craft or hobby shop.

2. Using a paper fastener, attach one "hand" to the center of a piece of tag board or cardboard cut to the size and shape needed.

3. Glue the necessary pictures to the edges and draw lines to separate each picture.

4. Remove the spinner to laminate and then reattach the spinner.

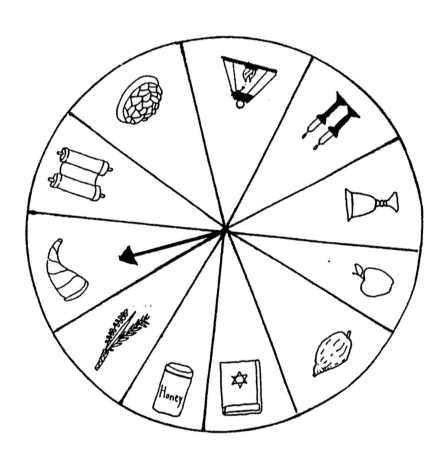

High Holiday Symbols

Apple

תַּפּוּחַ

ta-<u>poo</u>-ach

Synagogue בֵּית כְּנֶסֶת <u>beit</u> <u>kne</u>-set

Candles

נֵרוֹת

ne-<u>rot</u>

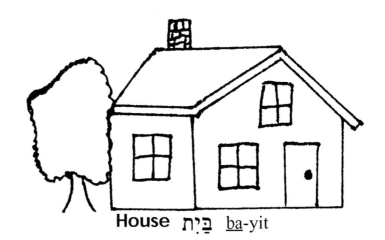

House בַּיִת <u>ba</u>-yit

Eternal Light

נֵר תָּמִיד

ner tamid

Etrog

אֶתְרוֹג

et-<u>rog</u>

Honey

דְּבַשׁ

<u>dvash</u>

High Holiday Symbols

Kiddush Cup

כּוֹס קָדוֹשׁ

<u>kos</u> ki-<u>doosh</u>

Lulav

לוּלָב

loo-<u>lav</u>

Round Challahs

חַלּוֹת עֲגוּלוֹת

cha-<u>lot</u> a -goo-<u>lot</u>

Shofar

שׁוֹפָר

sho-<u>far</u>

Prayer Book

סִדּוּר

si-dur

Torah

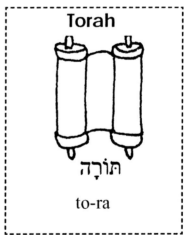

תּוֹרָה

to-ra

Game: "Peek-a-Boo, I See You"
(Matching High Holiday Symbols)

A GAME FOR THE HIGH HOLIDAYS

MATERIALS:
Single apple pattern*(p. 35)   "Hinged" apple pattern*(p. 35) Pencil pouch/envelope 11 High Holiday symbols* (from the HIGH HOLIDAY GAME: Apple, Candles, Round Challahs, Eternal Light, Etrog, Honey, Lulav, Kiddush Cup, Shofar, Siddur, Torah) (pp. 31, 32)

INSTRUCTIONS:
1. Copy 11 single apple patterns and 11 "hinged" apple patterns onto red paper.

2. Apply tape to the edge of the "hinged" apple if necessary, in order to keep them together.

3. Make two copies of the 11 High Holiday symbols. Color and cut out the pictures. The Hebrew and English words can be included to identify each object.

4. Glue one set of pictures onto the single apples, and one set of pictures onto the "hinged" apples.

5. Laminate all apple patterns. Be sure to laminate the "hinged" apple in an "open" position.

6. Fold "hinged" apples so the picture is not visible and the "hinged" apple is closed.

7. Store all apples in a pencil pouch or envelope.

DIRECTIONS TO PLAY "PEEK-A-BOO, I SEE YOU" GAME
(1-2 PLAYERS)

1. Place all the single apples face down on one side of the table and the closed "hinged" apples on the other.

2. Decide who will go first. A player turns over one single apple to reveal the picture. Then, the same player selects a "hinged" apple and opens it. If the two symbols match, this player says, "Peek-A-Boo, I See You" (the name of the symbol can be said as well). The player can keep the matching apples in front of them.

3. If the two symbols do not match, the apples are turned back and the next player goes.

4. Play continues until all the symbols have been matched.

EXAMPLE:

"Peek-a-Boo, I See You" Game Patterns

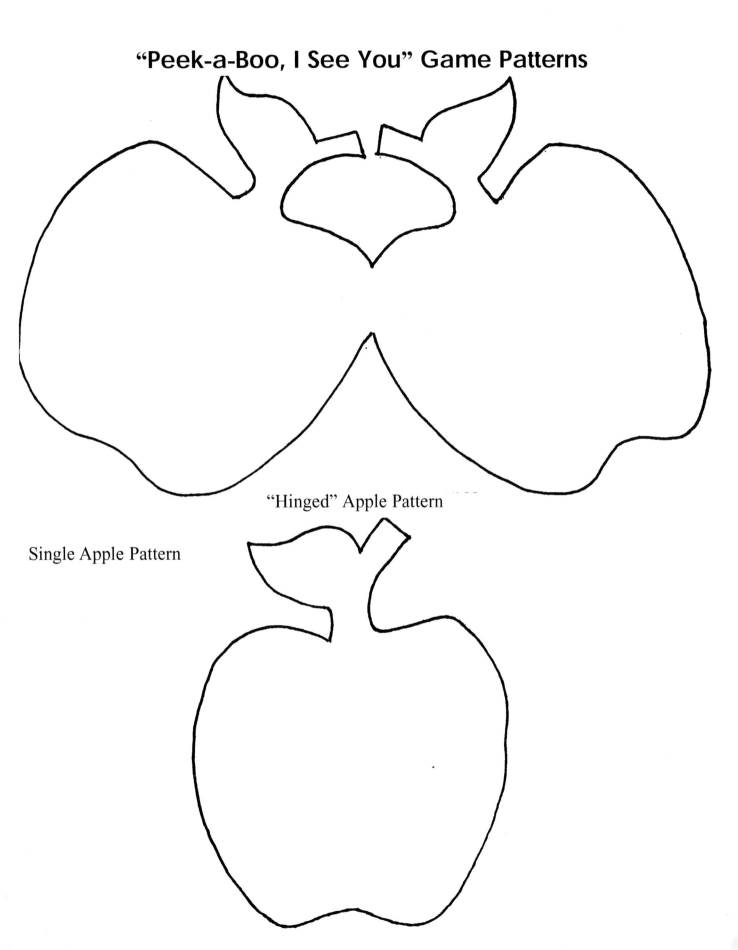

"Hinged" Apple Pattern

Single Apple Pattern

Game: Apple Number Match Game
(Math, Numbers 1-10)

A GAME FOR ROSH HASHANAH

MATERIALS:
Large apple pattern (p. 38)*   Small apple pattern*(p. 38)   File folder
Dot pattern suggestion (p. 38)   Pencil pouch or envelope

INSTRUCTIONS:
1. Copy the large apple pattern 10 times onto red paper.

2. Using the dot pattern suggestion, draw a seed pattern on each large apple. Color to look like half an apple.

3. Copy the small apple pattern 10 times onto white paper. Color to look like a whole apple.

4. Print one of the following on the small ("whole") apples: 1 one, 2 two, 3 three, 4 four, 5 five, 6 six, 7 seven, 8 eight, 9 nine, 10 ten.

5. Cut out all the apples.

6. Glue the large ("half") apples to the inside of the file folder.

7. Design a self-check on the back of the small ("whole") apples by drawing a dot pattern to match the seed pattern on the large ("half") apple.

8. Design a cover and glue the directions to the back of the file folder.

9. Laminate the file folder and small ("whole") apples.

10. Store the small ("whole") apples in a pencil pouch or envelope attached to the back of the folder.

DIRECTIONS TO PLAY APPLE NUMBER MATCH GAME
(ONE PLAYER)

1. The player removes the small ("whole") apples from the pencil pouch or envelope.

2. By counting the number of seeds on the large ("half") apple, the player will be able to place the correct small ("whole") apple on the large ("half") apple.

3. The player can check their own work by turning over the small ("whole") apples and checking the dot patterns to the seed patterns.

EXAMPLE:

Apple Number Match Patterns

Large Apple
(Half Apple)

Small Apple
(Whole Apple)

Dot Pattern Suggestion

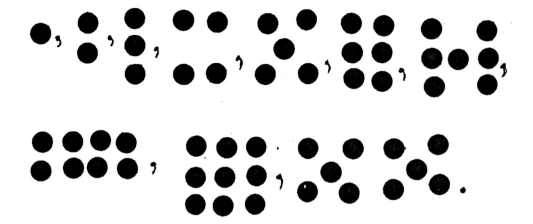

Game: Bear Honey Pot Matching Game
(Recognize High Holiday Symbols, Counting 1-10)

A GAME FOR THE HIGH HOLIDAYS

MATERIALS:
Bear pattern*(p. 41)   Honey pot pattern*(p. 41)   File Folder
10 Small Holiday symbols*(p. 41)   Pencil pouch or envelope

INSTRUCTIONS:
1. Copy the bear pattern ten times onto the colored paper of your choice, and cut out.

2. Glue the bears to the inside of the file folder.

3. Copy the honey pot pattern 10 times onto white paper. Color the top of the pot a honey color.

4. Copy the small Holiday symbols 10 times. Color and cut out the symbols.

5. Assign a symbol and an amount per bear. (Suggestion: 1 Torah, 2 Candles, 3 Lulavs, 4 Eternal Lights, 5 Apples, 6 Etrogs, 7 Jars of Honey, 8 Prayer Books, 9 Shofars, 10 Kiddush Cups.)

6. Glue the symbols to the bears.

7. On the honey pots write the following: one 1, two 2, three 3, four 4, five 5, six 6, seven 7, eight 8, nine 9, ten 10.

8. Design a self-check system on the back of the honey pots by gluing one symbol on the back of the honey pot that matches the one(s) on the bear.

9. Design a cover and glue the directions to the back of the file folder.

10. Laminate the file folder and honey pots.

11. Store the honey pots in a pencil pouch or envelope attached to the back of the file folder.

DIRECTIONS TO PLAY BEAR-HONEY POT MATCHING GAME
(ONE PLAYER)

1. The player removes the small ("whole") apples from the pencil pouch or envelope.

2. By counting the number of seeds on the large ("half") apple, the player will be able to place the correct small ("whole") apple on the large ("half") apple.

3. The player can check their own work by turning over the small ("whole") apples and checking the dot patterns to the seed patterns.

EXAMPLE:

Bear-Honey Pot Patterns and Symbols

| Apple | Candles | Eternal Light | Etrog | Jar of Honey |

| Kiddush Cup | Lulav | Prayer Book | Shofar | Torah |

Game: Bee and Beehive Game
(Matching Holiday Symbols, Fine Motor Development, Holiday Vocabulary)

A GAME FOR ROSH HASHANAH

MATERIALS:
Beehive and bee pattern*(p. 44)   Tag board   10 clothespins
10 Holiday pictures* (from the Bear Honey Pot Game) (p. 41)
Large manila envelope

INSTRUCTIONS:
1. Copy the beehive two times onto tag board.

2. Copy the bee ten times onto tag board.

3. Copy the Holiday pictures two times onto white paper.

4. Color and cut out the beehives, bees, and Holiday pictures.

5. Glue five Holiday pictures to the edge of one beehive. Glue the other five pictures to the edge of the other beehive.

6. Glue one Holiday picture to the body of each bee.

7. Laminate the beehives and bees.

8. Glue or staple one bee to the closed end of each clothespin.

9. Design a cover on the envelope and glue the directions to the back. Store the game pieces in the envelope.

DIRECTIONS TO PLAY BEE AND BEEHIVE GAME
(ONE PLAYER)

1. Remove the two beehives and the ten bees from the envelope.

2. The player matches the Holiday symbol on the bee by clipping the clothespin to the corresponding symbol on the beehive.

3. The player can say the name of the symbol as they clip the clothespin to the hive.

EXAMPLE:

Bee and Beehive Pattern

Dramatization: "How Bees Make Honey"

A SCIENCE ACTIVITY FOR ROSH HASHANAH

MATERIALS:
BEEKEEPER'S HAT — Cloth hat with netting attached to the hat's brim
WINGS FOR BEES — Cut WING PATTERN* (p. 47) from tag board, attach to sash.
SMALL MINI BASKET
2-3 ARTIFICIAL FLOWERS ON STEMS
PICTURE OF BEEHIVE — Use the picture of the Beehive (p. 44) and enlarge slightly.
HONEYCOMB (p. 48)
TOY CASH REGISTER
PLASTIC, EMPTY HONEY CONTAINER
WALLET OR BILLFOLD
PURSE OR POCKETBOOK

PARTS AND COSTUMES: *(Assign a child to play the following parts)*
BEEKEEPER *(wears hat and holds plastic container of honey)*
WORKER BEE *(wears wings and carries basket)*
GUARD BEE *(holds picture of beehive and wears wings)*
BEE *(holds honeycomb and wears wings)*
FLOWER GARDEN *(2-3 children hold flowers)*
STOREKEEPER *(uses cash register, sells honey)*
MALE AND FEMALE CUSTOMERS *(wallet and purse, purchase honey)*

THE TEACHER TELLS THE STORY AND HELPS THE CHILDREN ACT IT OUT.

The **Bees** live together in a **Beehive.** The **Worker Bee** flies to the **Flower Garden.** The **Bee** lands on a **Flower** and using its long tongue, drinks nectar from the **Flower.** Then the **Bee** flies to another **Flower** to get more nectar. The **Bee** stores the nectar in its **Stomach (Basket).** When its stomach is full, the **Bee** flies back to the **Hive** where it is recognized by the **Guard Bee** and allowed to enter the **Hive.** The **Bee** stores the nectar in the **Honeycomb Cells** with the help of the **Other Bees.** The nectar will become honey. Then the **Beekeeper** comes to the **Hive** wearing his protective clothing to gather the **Honey**. Then the **Beekeeper** sells the **Honey** to the **Storekeeper**. (Ask the "beekeeper" to tell the "storekeeper" how much money he wants for his honey.) Here the **Storekeeper** sells the **Honey** to the **Customers**. (Have the "storekeeper" tell the "customers" how much the honey costs.) The **Customers** take the **Honey** home to use with apples for Rosh Hashanah.

SOME ADDITIONAL INFORMATION ABOUT HONEYBEES

Honeybees are social insects and are helpful to plants. When bees fly from flower to flower, they collect a powder-like substance on their hind legs called *pollen* from the flowers. As the bee lands on each flower, some of the pollen brushes off onto the special parts of the flowers. Flowers need to have the pollen spread to these special parts so that they can make seeds, which will produce new flowers.

Bees have six legs, four wings, and a special stomach in which they carry nectar it has sucked up from flowers with its pipe-like tongue. All females have a stinger, which is used in self-defense.

A typical honeybee colony is made up of one queen, tens of thousands of sterile female worker bees, and a few hundred male drones. The drones have one purpose in life, to fertilize the queen. The fertilization process takes place during a mating flight high up in the air. Afterwards, the drones are starved and excluded or even forcibly removed from the hive.

Several worker bees guard the entrance to their hive. Because bees in each hive have their own special odor, the guard bees can detect bees from other colonies and thus attack these intruders.

When the bee returns to the hive with nectar and pollen, it is met by other bees that take the nectar from her. The bees pass the nectar back and forth swallowing and regurgitating it many times until it turns into honey. The honey is stored inside a cell which is sealed with a cap.

"How Bees Make Honey"
Wing Pattern

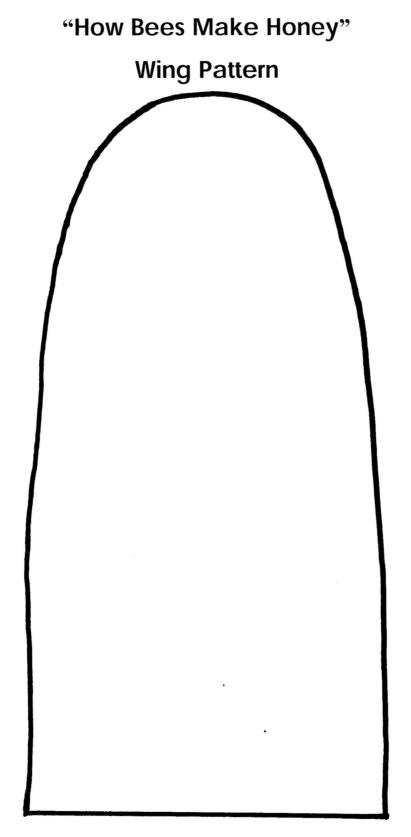

Place Pattern on fold at line and cut out to
make one pair of wings.

"How Bees Make Honey"

Honeycomb

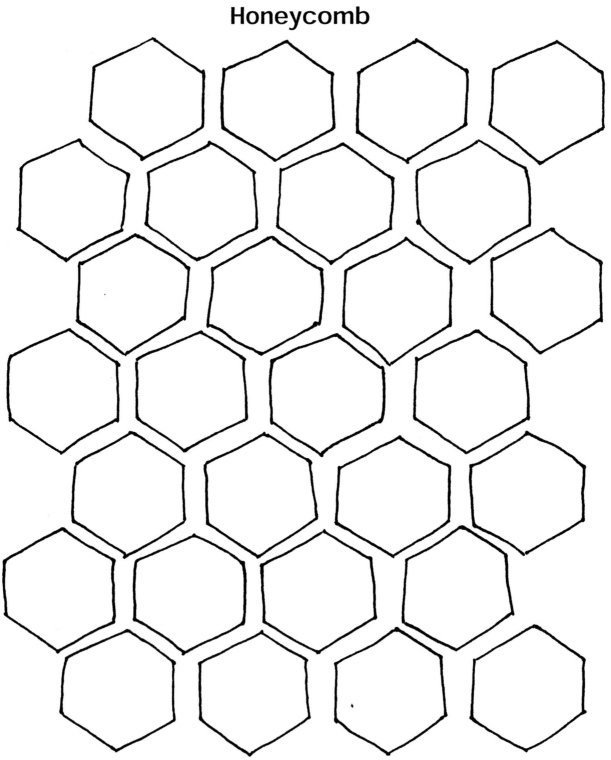

Dramatization: "The Story of Jonah"

A STORY FOR YOM KIPPUR

MATERIALS:
A large box big enough for one child to fit easily inside.

INSTRUCTIONS:
1. Have the children paint and decorate the box to be a big fish.

2. The children take turns being Jonah and being inside the big fish. The teacher can rock the box slightly to give the feeling of being inside a fish. Be sure to ask the child how they like being inside the "belly of a fish."

THE TEACHER TELLS THE STORY AND HELPS THE CHILDREN ACT IT OUT:

Once there was a man named Jonah. Jonah was a prophet and he lived in the land of Canaan. One day the Lord spoke to Jonah and said, "Go to Nineveh for the people there are wicked and they must learn to change their wicked ways." But Jonah did not want to go to Nineveh because he did not know the people there. So he went to the port city of Joppa, and bought a ticket on a boat that would take him far away from Nineveh. Once the boat was at sea the Lord sent a great storm that tossed the boat about in the sea. The sailors were afraid and threw overboard the goods they were carrying on the ship. But this did not help and the boat continued to be tossed about in the sea. During this time, Jonah had gone inside the ship and he was fast asleep. The captain came to Jonah and shouted, "How can you be sleeping through this storm? Wake up and pray to your God to save us." Jonah knew what he had to do. He had tried to run away from the Lord and the Lord had found him. Jonah told the sailors to throw him into the sea for then the sea would become calm. The sailors did not want to throw him overboard for they were afraid Jonah would die, but they did as Jonah asked. Then the Lord sent a great big fish to swallow Jonah for the Lord did not want Jonah to die and the sea became calm once again. Jonah stayed inside the great fish for three days and three nights. During this time Jonah prayed to the Lord for he knew that it was wrong to disobey Him. Then the Lord commanded the great fish to put Jonah out on the land again and told Jonah to go to Nineveh once again. This time Jonah obeyed the Lord and went directly to Nineveh. Jonah warned the people of

Nineveh they had 40 days to stop their wicked ways or the Lord would destroy the city. The people of Nineveh, from the oldest to the youngest, from the richest to the poorest, even the king heard Jonah's message and stopped their wicked ways and thus the Lord spared the city. However, Jonah was not pleased with the Lord's decision to spare the city. Jonah said to the Lord, "This is why I did not want to come to Nineveh. I knew you would change your mind for you are a good and compassionate God. I would rather die than live, so please Lord take my life now." The Lord said, "Are you right to be so angry?" So Jonah left the city and built a small shelter and sat down under it to watch the city. During the night the Lord sent a vine to grow over Jonah's shelter. All through the next day, the vine provided shade from the sun's heat. Jonah was happy with the vine. The next morning, the Lord sent a worm, which ate the plant so the vine died. Now the sun shone down on Jonah and made him feel faint. And Jonah said, "I would rather die than live." And the Lord said, "Are you right to be angry that the vine had died?" And Jonah answered, "Yes, I am right for the vine was a good thing." Then the Lord said to Jonah, "You cared about the vine which you did not plant and you did nothing to make it grow and it lived for just one day. Isn't the city of Nineveh with all the poeple in it much better than a vine?" And so Jonah learned that the Lord is everywhere and Jonah understood that the Lord is merciful, wise and forgiving too.

Note: This story of Jonah may contain more information than your students need. You may adjust htis story to fit the needs of your students.

Game: Decorate the Sukkah
(Matching Letters to Letters or Words to Words,
Naming Fruits and Objects in English and Hebrew)

A GAME FOR SUKKOT

MATERIALS:
English Sukkah pattern*(p. 52) Hebrew Sukkah pattern*(p. 54)
Fruit and object patterns* (Apple, Banana, Cherries, Etrog, Grapes, Lulav, Orange, Strawberry, Wine) in English and Hebrew (pp. 53, 55)

INSTRUCTIONS:
1. Decide if this game is to stress beginning sounds in English or Hebrew. Then copy that Sukkah pattern onto the inside of the file folder. (It may be necessary to enlarge the Sukkah to fit inside the file folder.)

2. Copy and color the fruit and object patterns in the chosen language.

3. Cut out the fruit and object pictures leaving the name under all the pictures.

4. Design a cover, and glue the directions to the back of the file folder.

5. Laminate the fruit and object pictures and the file folder.

6. Attach the pencil pouch or an envelope to the back of the folder to store all the game pieces.

DIRECTIONS TO PLAY DECORATE THE SUKKAH
(ONE PLAYER)

1. Remove the fruit and object pictures from the pencil pouch or envelope.

2. The player "hangs" or places each item in its proper place by matching the picture to its initial letter or Hebrew word.

3. When all the items have been placed, the Sukkah will be complete.

4. The player can name each item in the Sukkah.

English Sukkah Pattern

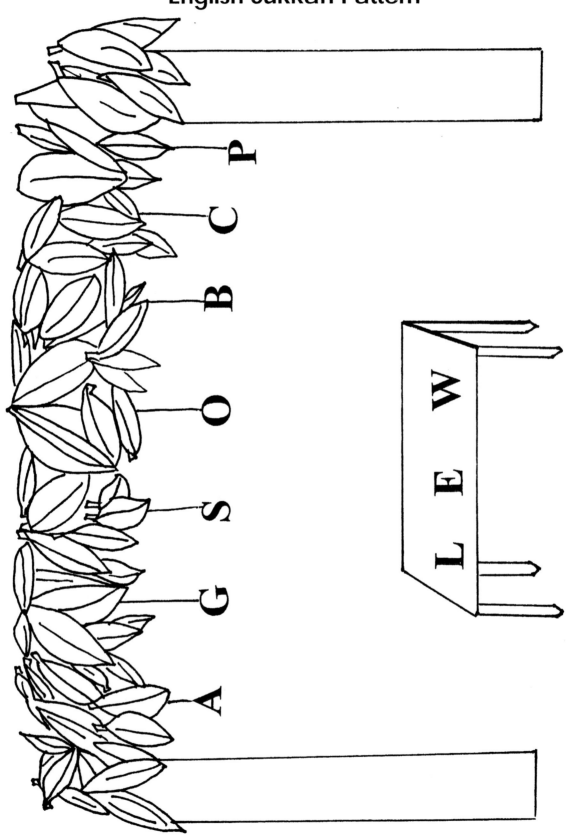

English Decorate the Sukkah Patterns

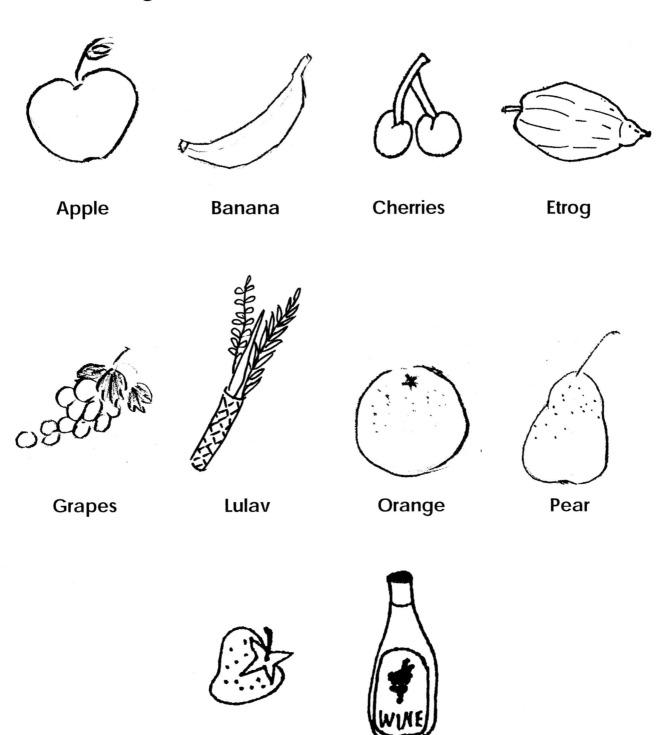

Apple Banana Cherries Etrog

Grapes Lulav Orange Pear

Strawberry Wine

Hebrew Sukkah Pattern

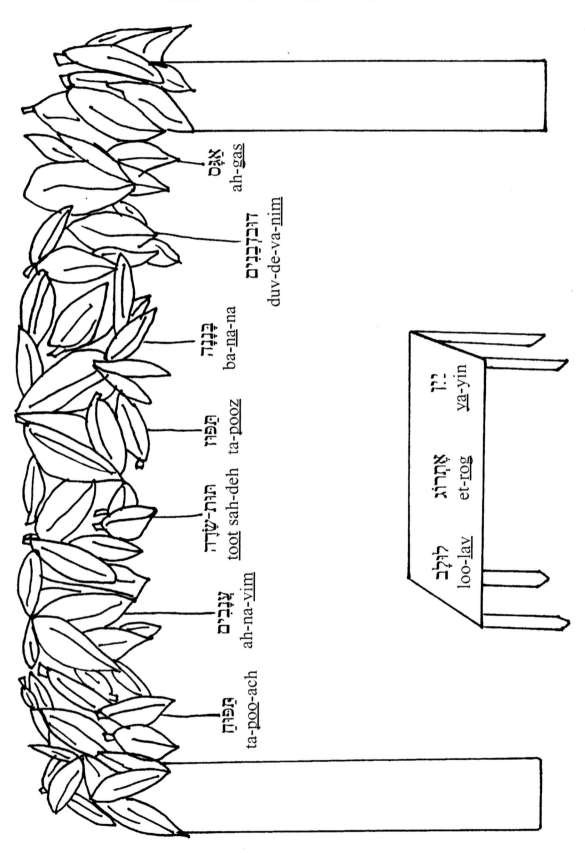

אֱגָס
ah-gas

דֻבְדְבָנִים
duv-de-va-nim

בָּנָנָה
ba-na-na

תַּפּוּז
ta-pooz

תוּת-שָׂדֶה
toot sah-deh

עֲנָבִים
ah-na-vim

תַּפּוּחַ
ta-poo-ach

יַיִן
ya-yin

אֶתְרוֹג
et-rog

לוּלָב
loo-lav

Hebrew Decorate the Sukkah Patterns

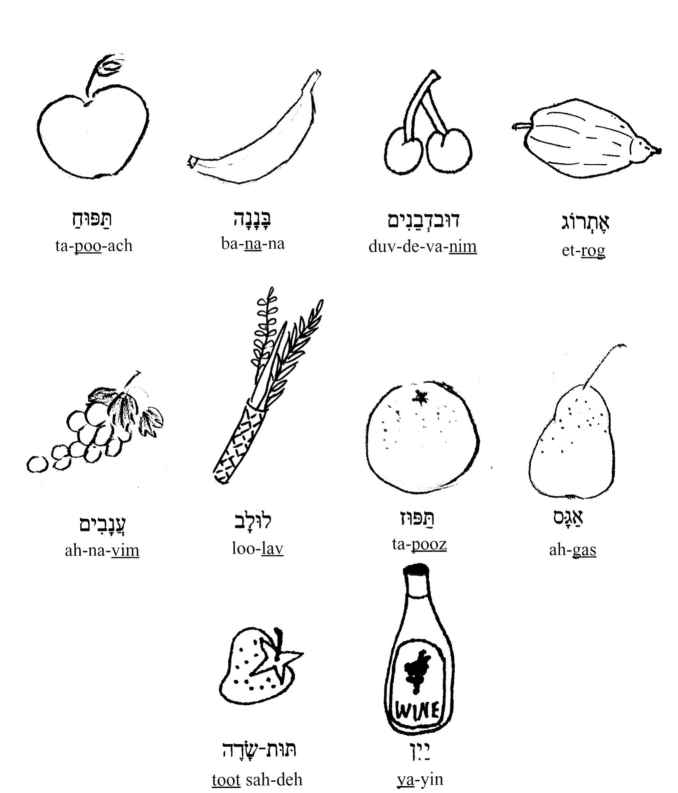

תַּפּוּחַ
ta-<u>poo</u>-ach

בָּנָנָה
ba-<u>na</u>-na

דוּבְדְבָנִים
duv-de-va-<u>nim</u>

אֶתְרוֹג
et-<u>rog</u>

עֲנָבִים
ah-na-<u>vim</u>

לוּלָב
loo-<u>lav</u>

תַּפּוּז
ta-<u>pooz</u>

אַגָּס
ah-<u>gas</u>

תּוּת-שָׂדֶה
<u>toot</u> sah-deh

יַיִן
<u>ya</u>-yin

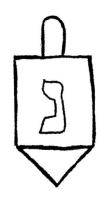

CHANUKAH

Background Information for the Chanukah

WORDS TO KNOW:

Chanukah: A festival Holiday beginning on the evening of the 25th day of Kislev and ends on the third of Tevet on the Jewish calendar. The holiday lasts for eight days. Chanukah means "rededication."

Chanukiah: A nine-branch candleholder where one shaft is designed for the *shammash* (the servant candle), which is used to light the other candles.

Dreidel: A Yiddish word that means *sevivon* in Hebrew. A spinning top with four Hebrew letters (Nunב , Gimmelג , Heyה , Shinש) which in Hebrew stands for "Nes Gadol Hayah Sham" and means "A Great Miracle Happened There." According to legend, the top was used during the time of Maccabees when Antiochus forbade the study of Torah. Jewish people would gather secretly to study the Torah and if the soldiers approached, all they would see was Jews playing an innocent game of "dreidel."

Gelt: Money. Today gelt is gold foil covered chocolate candy.

Gift: A modern way to celebrate Chanukah with the giving of gifts to family and friends.

Jug of Oil: When the Holy Temple was restored in Jerusalem, the Maccabees found one jug of pure oil, enough to last for one day. A miracle happened and the oil burned for eight days.

Latkes: A Yiddish word for pancakes made from potatoes and fried in oil. The oil symbolizes the miracle of the jug of oil that lasted for eight days.

Maccabee: A Hebrew word meaning "hammer." Judah, the leader of the revolt against the Syrian Greek army, became known as "Judah the Maccabee" or "Judah the Hammer" because of his great strength and strategy abilities during the fight for religious freedom.

BACKGROUND:

Chanukah is a festival Holiday that commemorates a time when a small band of heroic Jews, led by Judah Maccabee and his four brothers, won their religious freedom against the Syrian Greeks under Antiochus IV, king of Syria, in the year 165 B.C.E.

King Antiochus outlawed Judaism forbidding reading from the Torah, celebrating Shabbat, festivals and holy days. Antiochus also forced the Jews to bow down to idols of Greek gods. When the Syrian officials and soldiers came to the town of Modin, a priest named Mattahias and his five sons refused to pay taxes and worship the idols. They banded together with other followers and killed the Syrian officials and soldiers. Thus began the revolt against the Syrian Greeks. Eventually the Maccabees defeated the Syrian Greek army and were able to return to Jerusalem and reclaim the defiled and desecrated Temple. The Jews immediately began to clean their Temple, in order to rededicate themselves to God and their faith. One jug of pure oil was found to light the Eternal Light. Thinking this oil would only last for one day it miraculously lasted for eight days, enough time for the priests to make more pure oil.

Chanukah lasts for eight days reminding us of the one-day supply of pure oil that burned for eight days when the Temple was rededicated. Today we light candles on a Chanukiah beginning with one candle on the first night and adding one more on each consecutive night of Chanukah. A helper candled, called a shammash, is lit first and is used to light the other candles. We eat latkes and spin the dreidel to celebrate the holiday.

Game: Latkes Frying in the Pan
(Counting, Matching Numbers 1-10)

A GAME FOR CHANUKAH

MATERIALS:

Frying pan pattern*(p. 62)	"Latke" patterns*(p. 63)	Tag board
Brown construction paper	Large manila envelope	Small envelope

INSTRUCTIONS:

1. Copy the frying pan pattern ten times onto tag board and cut out.

2. Copy the "latke" pattern onto brown construction paper three times and cut out. (Note: only 55 "latkes" are needed for the game. By making three copies, there will be extra in case some are lost.)

3. On the frying pan, write the following: 1 one, 2 two, 3 three, 4 four, 5 five, 6 six, 7 seven, 8 eight, 9 nine, 10 ten.

4. Design a self-check dot pattern on the handle of each pan. (See APPLE NUMBER MATCH GAME for dot pattern suggestions) (p. 38).

5. Laminate all pieces.

6. Design a cover for the large manila envelope and glue the directions to the back. Keep the "latkes" in the small envelope. Store all pieces in the large manila envelope.

DIRECTIONS TO PLAY LATKES FRYING IN THE PAN
(ONE PLAYER)

1. The player places the frying pans on the table.

2. The player will put the correct number of "latkes" on each frying pan.

3. The player can check their own work by checking the dots on the handle and seeing if the dots correspond to the number of "latkes" in the pan.

Frying Pan Pattern

"Latke" Patterns

Game: Mail Delivery Game
(Math — 1-10 Correspondence, Number Recognition)

A GAME FOR CHANUKAH

MATERIALS:

House Pattern*(p. 66)   Envelope Patterns*(p. 67)

INSTRUCTIONS:

1. Copy the house pattern onto tag board 10 times.

2. Cut out the 10 houses. Fold on the dotted line and tape the edges together.

3. Draw windows and a door on each house. Write a numeral 1-10 on the "roof" of each house.

4. A self-check can be designed on the back of each house so the player can check their work. (Another self-check suggestion: design a self-check by drawing small flowers on either side of the door to correspond to the number on the "roof".)

5. Laminate each house; cut a slit along the folded edge.

6. Make 55 pieces of "mail" and cut out. Laminate if desired. Store "mail" in a small envelope.

7. On a large manila envelope, design a cover and glue the directions to the back. Store all the pieces in the large envelope.

DIRECTIONS TO PLAY MAIL DELIVERY GAME
(ONE PLAYER)

1. Remove all the houses and "mail" envelope from the large manila envelope.

2. The player will place the proper number of "mail" in the slit of each house corresponding to the numeral on the "roof."

3. The player can use the self-check to check their work.

EXAMPLE:

Cut Slit

Mail Delivery House Pattern

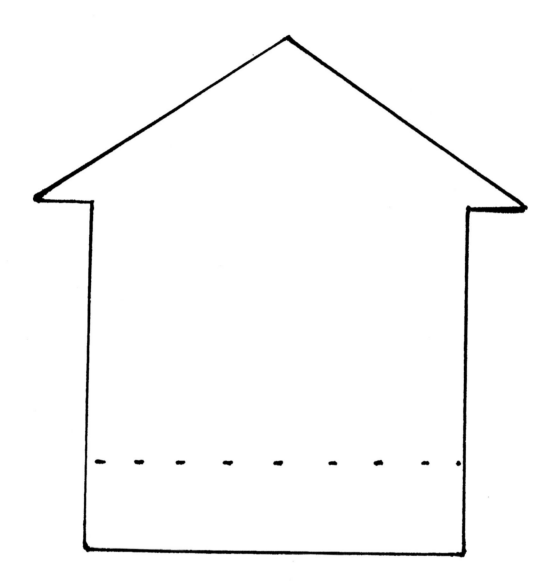

Mail Delivery Envelope Patterns

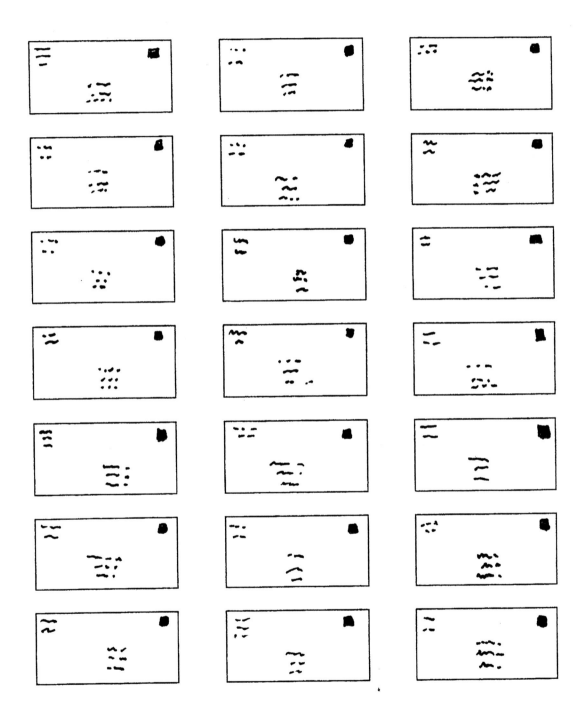

Game: Chanukah Board Game
(Matching Pictures, Chanukah Objects in English and Hebrew)

A GAME FOR CHANUKAH

MATERIALS:
Large folder   Chanukah "die" pattern*(p. 71)   Tag board
6 Chanukah symbols* (Candle, Chanukiah, Dreidel, Gelt, Gift, Jug of Oil) (p. 70)
4 Movers   Pencil pouch

INSTRUCTIONS:
1. Copy the Chanukah symbols seven times. Color and cut out the pictures.

2. Draw a rectangle in the lower left corner of the file folder. Write the word "START" inside the rectangle.

3. In the upper right corner draw a rectangle and write the word "HOME" inside the rectangle. Place a picture inside the "HOME" rectangle for a final move.

4. Using the Chanukah pictures, design a snake-like path from "START" to "HOME", varying the pictures.

5. Design a cover for the file folder and glue the directions to the back.

6. Copy the "die" pattern onto tag board. Color the pictures.

7. Laminate the "die" pattern and file folder.

8. Cut out the "die" pattern cutting along the dotted lines. Put the "die" together to form a cube by folding on the solid lines. Tape the edges together.

9. Store the movers and "die" inside a pencil pouch. Attach the pouch to the back of the folder.

OPTIONAL: A discarded game board and/or spinner can be used to create this game. See the HIGH HOLIDAY GAME (p. 28) for instructions.

DIRECTIONS TO PLAY CHANUKAH BOARD GAME
(2-4 PLAYERS)

1. Players select a mover and place it on "START".

2. Decide who will go first. The first player rolls the "die" and then moves to the matching symbol.

3. Play continues in this manner to all players.

4. If the "die" lands on a symbol that is not in front of the player, the player doesn't move and play continues to the next player.

5. As each player reaches "HOME" they say HAPPY CHANUKAH! (or "חֲנֻכָּה שָׂמֵחַ" (cha-nu-ka sa-<u>mei</u>-ach) in Hebrew.) Play continues until all players reach "HOME".

Chanukah Board Game Symbols

Candle

נֵר

ner

Dreidel

סְבִיבוֹן

se-vi-<u>von</u>

(spinning top)

Gift

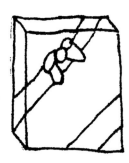

מַתָּנָה

ma-ta-<u>na</u>

Chanukiah

חֲנוּכִּיָּה

cha-noo-ki-<u>ya</u>

Gelt

מָעוֹת

ma-<u>ot</u>

(money)

Jug of Oil

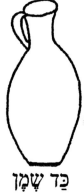

כַּד שֶׁמֶן

<u>ka</u> <u>she</u>-men

Chanukah Game "Die" Pattern

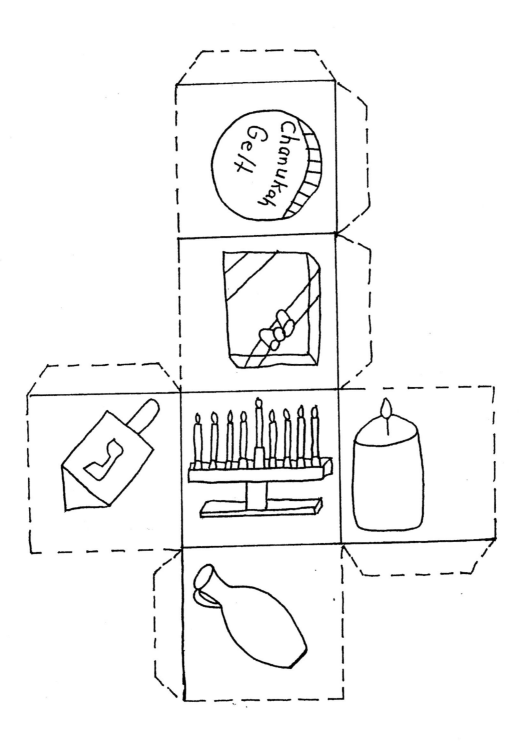

Tu B'Shevat

Background Information for Tu B'Shevat

WORDS TO KNOW:

Tu B'Shevat: The fifteenth of Shevat, the Birthday or New Year of the Trees.

BACKGROUND:

Tu B'Shevat, the New Year or Birthday of the Trees, on the Jewish calendar it falls on the fifteenth of Shevat which is the first day of Spring in Israel. In North America the holiday falls in either late January or February. Through a Tu B'Shevat Seder, people eat foods (such as dates, figs, oranges, and nuts) that are grown in Israel.

Art: Family Tree
(Art Idea)

FOR TU B'SHEVAT

MATERIALS:

Tree pattern*(p. 77)   Leaf patterns*(pp. 78, 79)   Tag board or cardboard

INSTRUCTIONS:

1 Copy several tree patterns onto tag board or cardboard and cut out.

2. Make a variety of leaf patterns onto tag board or cardboard using all or a few of the patterns provided. (The names of the leaves have been provided for easy identification.)

3. The child uses the tree pattern and traces it onto brown construction paper. The child cuts out the tree and glues it to another sheet of paper.

4. The child takes a leaf pattern and traces it onto a piece of colored construction paper of their choice.

5. The child makes one leaf for each member of their family, who lives in their home.

6. The child cuts out the leaves and glues them on the tree's branches.

7. Write the names of the family members on the leaves.

EXAMPLE:

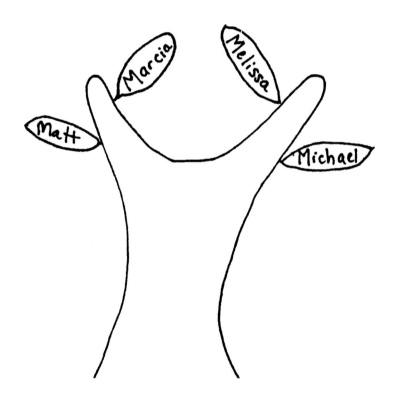

Family Tree Pattern

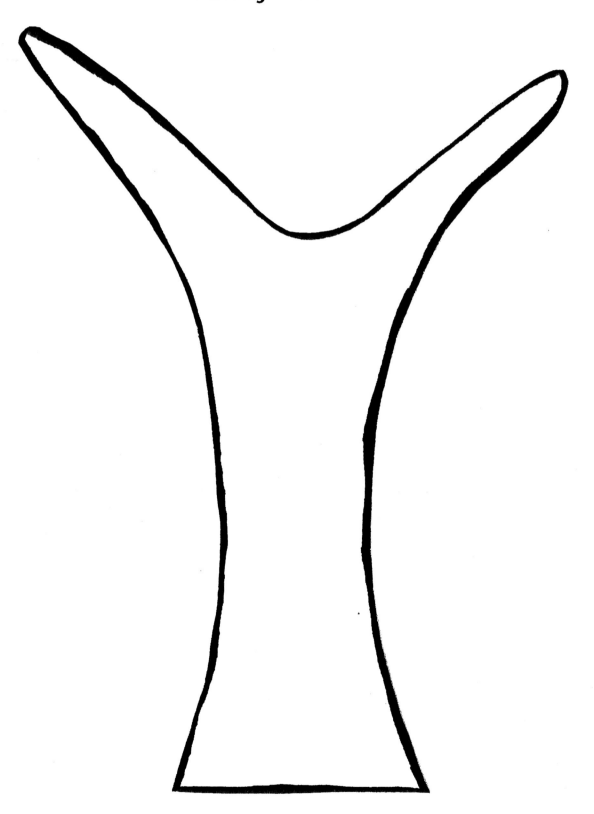

Family Tree Leaf Patterns

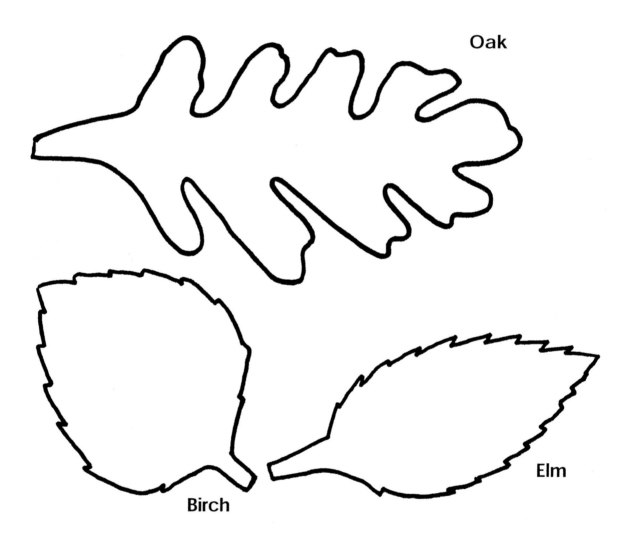

Family Tree Leaf Patterns

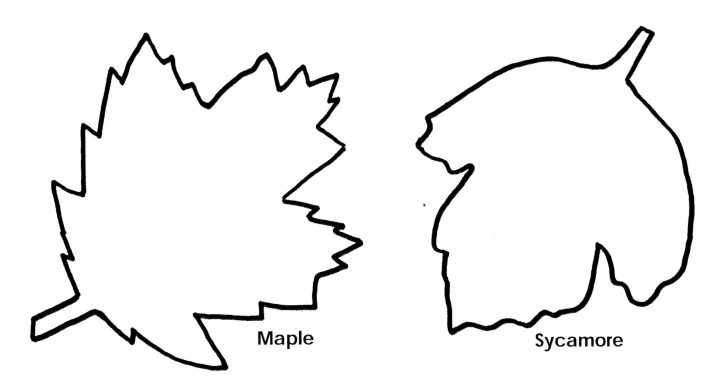

Maple

Sycamore

PURIM

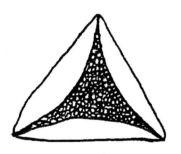

Background Information for Purim

WORDS TO KNOW:
PURIM CHARACTERS:
King Ahasuerus: Ruled over Persia from the capital city of Shushan.

Queen Vashti: The King's first wife who refused to appear before him at a palace party and as a result was killed.

Esther: A very beautiful Jewish maiden who was picked by King Ahasuerus to be his new Queen. Esther is the heroine of the story.

Mordecai: Esther's relative, either an uncle or a cousin who raised her as his own daughter. (In this text, the author has chosen to refer to Mordecai as Esther's uncle.)

Haman: The King's chief advisor and the evil "villain" of the story of Purim. He wanted to kill all the Jews of Persia and picked the fourteenth day of Adar for the pogrom.

Crown: Represents the crown King Ahasuerus placed on Esther's head when he made her his queen. Also used when children dress in costumes to celebrate Purim.

Grogger: A noisemaker, used to drown out the name of Haman when the Megillah is read in synagogue.

Hamantashen: A Yiddish word for a triangle-shaped fruit filled cookie. The Hamantashen has several symbolic meanings. It could represent Haman's 3-cornered hat, Haman's pockets, or Haman's ears.

Mask: Purim is a jovial festival full of fun and merrymaking. This frivolity led to masquerading once a forbidden activity because it often involved men and women interchanging clothes. However, since Purim is such a joyous festival, the Rabbis allowed this breach of biblical law. Also used when children dress in costumes to celebrate Purim.

Megillah: The scroll, which contains the "Story of Purim," also known as the "Book of Esther."

Purim: A festival Holiday. When Haman plotted to kill the Jews of Persia, he cast "lots" (Purim) to pick a day (the 14th of Adar).

Shalach Manot: The exchange of fruit, cookies, and other treats among friends and neighbors. The words "Shalach Manot" mean "sending gifts."

BACKGROUND:

Purim is a festival holiday that falls on the 14th day of Adar in the Jewish calendar, which occurs in late February or early March in the secular calendar. The holiday begins with the reading of the Megillah, which contains the story of Queen Esther, wife of Ahasuerus, King of Persia, who ruled in the 5th century B.C.E. Esther's uncle, Mordecai, a good Jew, refused to bow down before Haman, the King's Prime Minister. Haman went to the King with a plot to kill all the Jews. Esther went before King Ahasuerus and revealed that she was Jewish and thus she too would be killed. King Ahasuerus then ordered Haman to be hanged on the gallows he had built for Mordecai and the Jews. Then Ahasuerus made Mordecai his advisor.

Today, when the Megillah is read in synagogue, groggers (noisemakers) are used to drown out the name of Haman. Children dress in costumes as King Ahasueus, Queen Esther, Uncle Mordecai, or Haman. Gifts are exchanged (Shalah Manot) and Hamantashens are eaten.

Game: Purim Board Game
(Matching Pictures, Names of Purim Objects in English and Hebrew)

A GAME FOR PURIM

MATERIALS:

Large file folder	Purim "die" pattern*(p. 87)	Tag board
Pencil pouch	4 Movers	

6 Purim symbols* (Crown, Grogger, Hamantashan, Mask, Megillah, Shalach Manot Basket) (p. 86)

INSTRUCTIONS:

1. Copy the Purim symbols seven times. Color and cut out all the pictures.

2. Draw a rectangle in the lower left corner of the file folder. Write the word "START" inside the rectangle.

3. In the upper right corner draw a rectangle and write the word "HOME" inside the rectangle.

4. Using the Purim pictures, design a snake-like path from "START" to "HOME" varying the pictures. Place a picture inside the "HOME" rectangle as a final move.

5. Design a cover for the file folder and glue the directions to the back.

6. Copy the "die" pattern onto tag board. Color the pictures.

7. Laminate the "die" pattern and the file folder.

8. Cut out the "die" pattern cutting along the dotted lines. Put the "die" together to form a cube folding on the solid lines. Tape the edges together.

9. Store the movers and "die" inside a pencil pouch. Attach the pouch to the back of the folder.

OPTIONAL: A discarded gameboard and/or spinner can be used to create this game. See the HIGH HOLIDAY GAME (p. 28) for instructions.

DIRECTIONS TO PLAY PURIM BOARD GAME
(ONE PLAYER)

1. Players select a mover and place it on "START."

2. Decide who will go first. The first player rolls the "die" and then moves to the matching symbol.

3. Play continues in this manner to all players.

4. If the "die" lands on a symbol that is not in front of the player, the player does not move and play continues to the next player.

5. As each player reaches "HOME," they say, "HAPPY PURIM!" (or "פּוּרִים שָׂמֵחַ" (pu-rim sa-mei-ach) in Hebrew.) Play continues until all players reach "HOME."

Purim Board Game Symbols

Crown

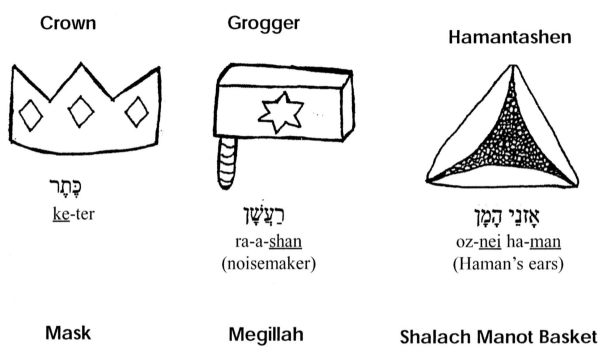

כֶּתֶר

ke-ter

Grogger

רַעֲשָׁן

ra-a-shan

(noisemaker)

Hamantashen

אָזְנֵי הָמָן

oz-nei ha-man

(Haman's ears)

Mask

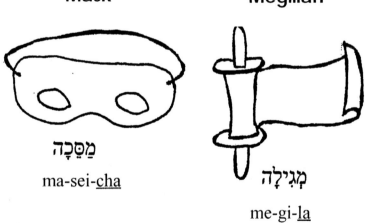

מַסֵּכָה

ma-sei-cha

Megillah

מְגִילָה

me-gi-la

Shalach Manot Basket

סַל מִשְׁלוֹחַ מָנוֹת

sal mish-lo-ach ma-not

Purim Game "Die" Pattern

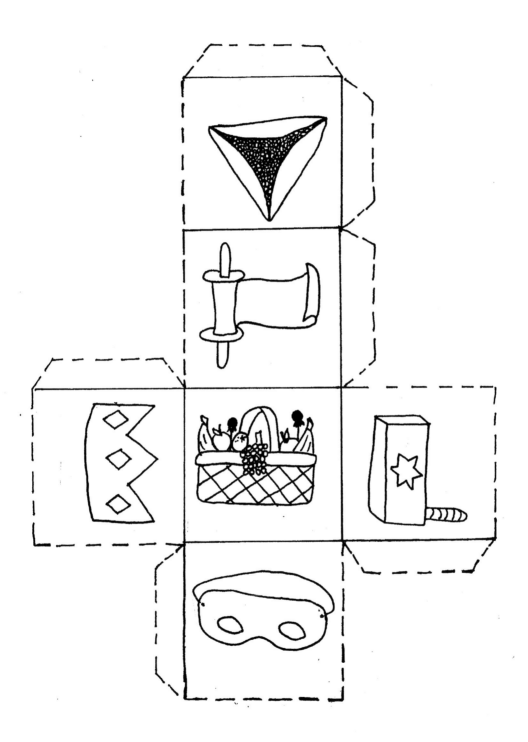

Game: Fill the Shalach Manot Basket
(Matching Colors, Names of Colors, Foods, and Haman)

A GAME FOR PURIM*

MATERIALS:
Basket pattern*(p. 91)   File folder   Die
House and Synagogue pattern*(from High Holiday Game) (p.31)
Pictures of food*(Apple, Banana, Grapes, Hamantashen, Orange, Pear) (p. 91)
Haman's face*(p. 91)   1" white self-adhesive circles   Pencil pouch
4 movers

INSTRUCTIONS:
1. Copy the pictures of the House and the Synagogue. Color and cut out.

2. Place the House in the lower left corner of the file folder.

3. Place the Synagogue in the upper right corner of the file folder.

4. Copy the picture of Haman's face 5-6 times and cut each into a 1" circle.

5. Color 5-6 self-adhesive circles one of each color - red, yellow, purple, brown, orange, and green.

6. From the House to the Synagogue, make a snake-like path alternating the different colored 1" circles and Haman's face. Place one circle on the Synagogue as a final move.

7. Copy the basket 4 times and color each its own color. Cut out the baskets.

8. Copy the food pictures 24 times. Color the food pieces the following: Apples-red, Bananas-yellow, Grapes-purple, Hamantashen-brown, Oranges-orange, Pears-green. Cut out all the food pieces.

9. Design a cover for the file folder and glue the directions to the back.

10. Laminate the file folder, baskets, and all the food pieces.

11. Attach a pencil pouch to the back of the file folder. Store all the food pieces, baskets, movers and die inside.

*This game may require teacher supervision.

DIRECTIONS TO PLAY FILL THE SHALACH MANOT BASKET
(2-4 PLAYERS)

1. Each player selects a basket. Each player selects a mover and places it on the House. Keep the food pieces in the pencil pouch.

2. Decide who will go first. The first player rolls the die and moves the proper number of spaces.

3. If the player lands on a color, they select one piece of food of that color and put it on their basket.

4. If a player lands on Haman, they must put one piece of food, of their choice, back into the pencil pouch. (If the first roll lands on Haman, the player's turn is over.)

5. Play continues in this manner to all players.

6. All players who reach the Synagogue can say, "HAPPY PURIM!" (or "פּוּרִים שָׂמֵחַ" (pu-rim sa-mei-ach) in Hebrew.)

*This game may require teacher supervision.

Fill the Shalach Manot Basket Game Key

(Color each square its appropriate color)

KEY:

☐ Red=Apples   ☐ Yellow=Bananas

☐ Purple=Grapes   ☐ Brown= Hamantashens

☐ Orange=Oranges   ☐ Green=Pears

Fill the Shalach Manot Basket Game Pieces

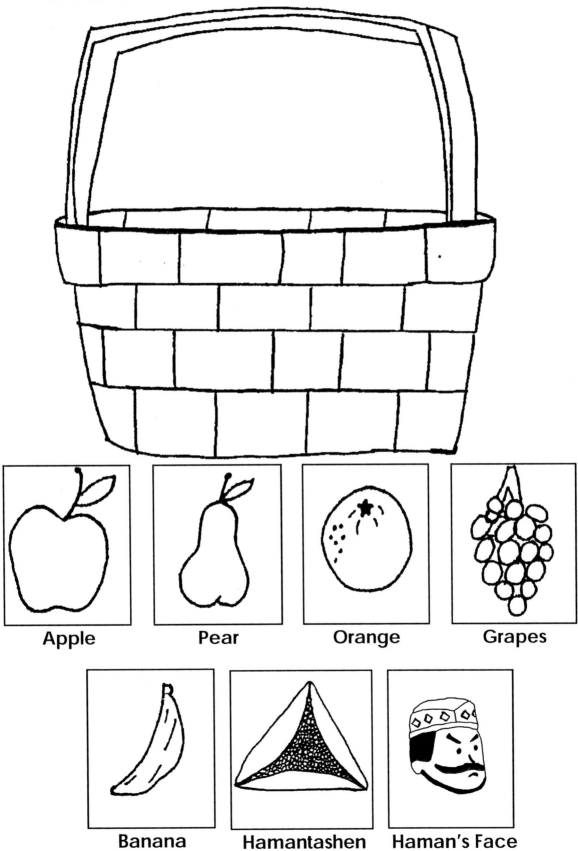

Apple   Pear   Orange   Grapes

Banana   Hamantashen   Haman's Face

Art: Gelatin Box Grogger

MATERIALS:

Empty gelatin or pudding box   White paper   Tape
Beans or buttons   Large craft sticks   Glue

DIRECTIONS:

1. Place a few beans or buttons inside an empty gelatin or pudding box.

2. Place the craft stick over the opening, leaving one end of the stick as the handle, tape closed.

3. Wrap the box in white paper, gluing down.

4. Make enough for each student. The children can decorate their own groggers.

EXAMPLE:

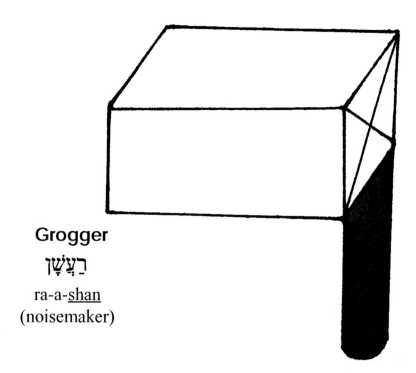

Grogger

רַעֲשָׁן

ra-a-<u>shan</u>

(noisemaker)

Purim, Purim What Do You See?
(Counting 1-8, Names of Purim Objects)

A COUNTING RHYME FOR PURIM

MATERIALS:
9 Pages to "Purim, Purim What Do You See?"*

INSTRUCTIONS:
1. Copy and color the 9 pages to "Purim, Purim What Do You See?"

2. Laminate, and bind the pages into a "book" form.

Purim, Purim

What Do You See?

By Marcia Shemaria Green

Purim, Purim what do you see?

I see...

1 Megillah looking at me!

Purim, Purim what do you see?

I see...

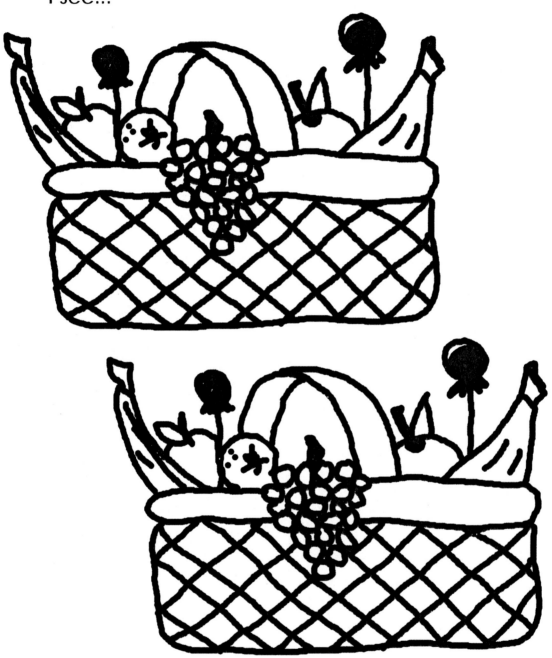

2 Shalah Manot Baskets looking at me!

Purim, Purim what do you see?

I see...

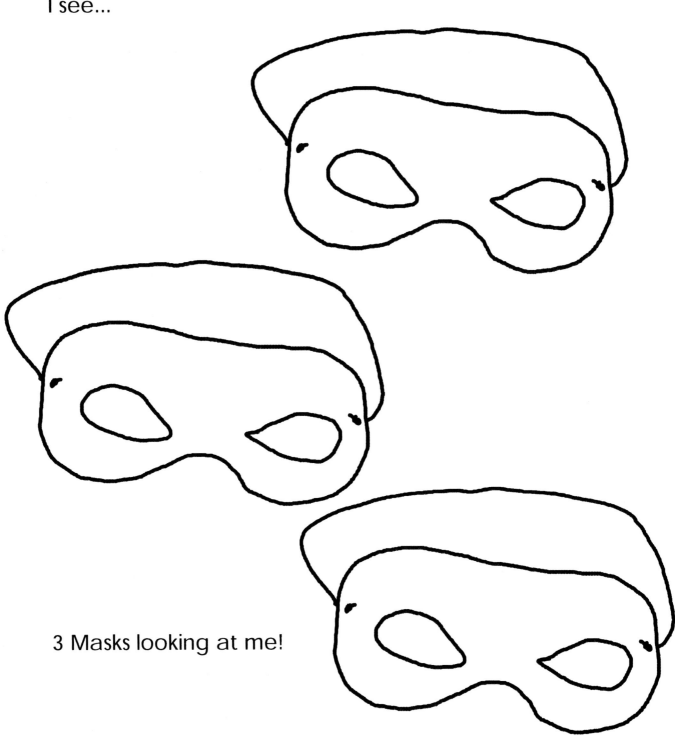

3 Masks looking at me!

Purim, Purim what do you see?

I see....

4 Costumes looking at me!

Purim, Purim what do you see?

I see...

5 Purim Characters looking at me! (King Ahasuerus, Queen Vashti, Haman, Uncle Mordecai, Queen Esther)

Purim, Purim what do you see?

I see...

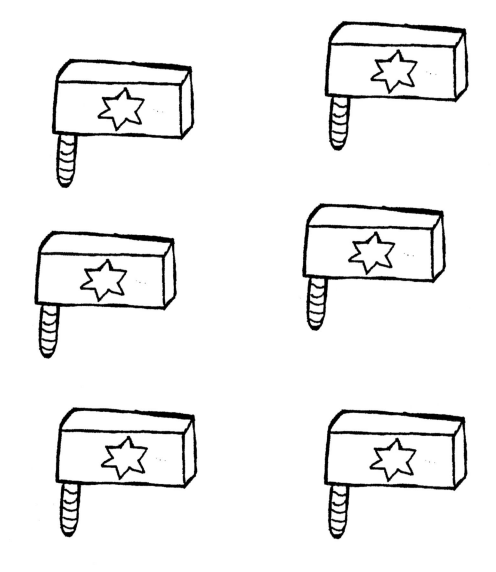

6 Groggers looking at me!

Purim, Purim what do you see?

I see...

7 Crowns looking at me!

Purim, Purim what do you see?

I see...

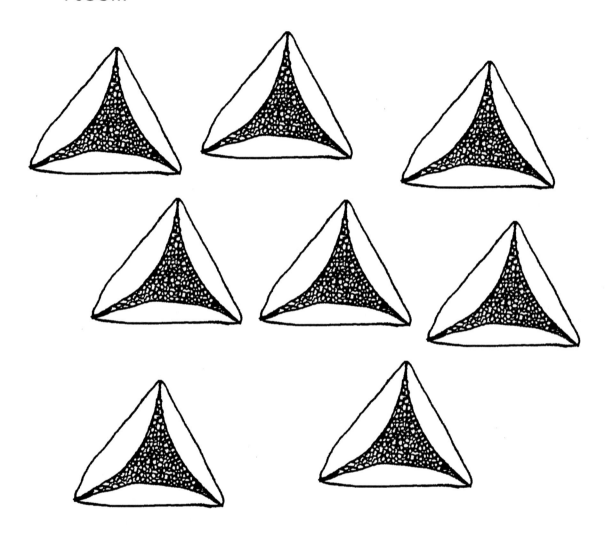

8 Hamantashens looking at me!

PASSOVER

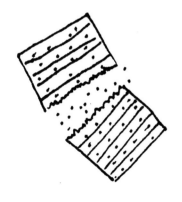

Background Information for Passover

WORDS TO KNOW:

Afikomen: Three whole matzahs that are placed one above the other, separated by a cloth or napkin, on the table. During a specific part in the Seder the middle matzah is broken in half. One half of this matzah is eaten and the other half becomes the "afikomen." The "afikomen" is hidden by the leader of the Seder and the child who finds it is usually given a present, for the "afikomen" is eaten as dessert. Afikomen is a Greek word that means "dessert."

Burning Bush: Through a vision of a burning bush that wasn't consumed by fire, Moses was told by God to go down to Egypt and tell Pharaoh to let the slaves go free.

Candles: As with every Shabbat and festival, candles are placed on the table and lit and blessed by a female just before the Seder begins.

Four Questions: The youngest school aged child at the Seder table recites the four questions pertaining to the Story of Passover. The four questions are found in the Haggadah.

Frogs: Part of the 10 plagues the Lord sent to punish Pharaoh and the Egyptians. The Israelites were not afflicted or inconvenienced by these plagues. The order of the plagues is: blood, frogs, lice, flies, cattle disease, boils, hail, locust, darkness, and the slaying of the firstborn. After the tenth plague when Pharaoh's own son died, Pharaoh allowed the Israelites to leave.

Haggadah: The Haggadah (from the Hebrew *hagged*, which means "to tell") is used as a guidebook for the celebration of Passover, containing directions on how to conduct the Seder, explanations of the Passover symbols, and tells the story of why we celebrate Passover.

Matzah: Flat, unleavened bread eaten during the holiday of Passover. When Pharaoh finally let the Israelites go, they left in a hurry and did not have time to wait for their bread to rise. Carrying the dough on pieces of wood tied to their shoulders, the hot sun baked the unleavened dough into matzah.

Moses: The Jewish leader who led his people out of Egypt.

Open the Door: (for Elijah) A special cup of wine is set on the table for the prophet

Elijah. We open the door to symbolically welcome Elijah as well as others to the table.

Passover: A springtime holiday and a pilgrimage festival, celebrating the Exodus from Egypt when Moses led the Jewish people out of slavery. Passover begins in the evening with the first full moon in Spring, on the 14th of the Jewish month of Nisan and is observed for eight days. Thus the first day of Passover falls on the 15th day of the Jewish month of Nisan.

Pharaoh: The ruler or king of Egypt.

Pyramid: A quadrilateral stone monument, built by the slaves and used as a tomb for Pharaoh.

Seder: In Hebrew, Seder means "order" or "arrangement." A ritual dinner eaten during the first and/or second night of Passover which includes the reading of the Haggadah, the eating of certain foods that are symbolic of the Israelites' bondage in Egypt and of the Exodus, as well as singing of traditional songs.

Seder Plate: A dish containing the symbolic Seder foods (bitter herbs, green herbs, haroset, lamb bone, roasted egg) used during the meal.

> *The meaning of the symbolic foods on the Seder Plate:*
>
> *Bitter Herbs (Maror)*: Usually horseradish represents the bitterness of slavery.
>
> *Green Herbs (Karpas)*: The Greens (lettuce, parsley or celery) represent Spring, the season when Passover appears. The Green Herbs are dipped into salt water to remind us of the salty tears the slaves wept. The salt water is placed next to the Seder plate.
>
> *Haroset*: A mixture of apples, nuts, cinnamon, and wine that represents the mortar made by the slaves to build Pharaoh's cities, palaces, and pyramids.
>
> *Lamb bone (shank bone)*: The shank bone is a reminder that "the Lord brought us forth with a strong hand and an outstretched arm" thus the bone represents the "arm." A roasted bone also represents the Paschal lamb that was sacrificed at the Temple of our ancestors. The lamb bone was used to mark the Israelites homes with blood so that the "Angel of Death" passed over their homes when He

smote the Egyptians and spared the Israelites.

Roasted Egg: The egg is a traditional symbol of mourning, and as a sign of our mourning of the destruction of the ancient Temple. The egg can also represent the beginning of a new life.

Slaves: Pharaoh enslaved the Jewish people to build new cities, palaces and pyramids.

Wine: According to the order mentioned in the Hagaddah, we are instructed when to drink the four cups of wine during the Seder. There are four cups because in the Book of Exodus in the Torah, the Lord's promise to free the Israelites from slavery is repeated four times: 1. "I will bring you out of Egypt." 2. "I will deliver you from their bondage." 3. "I will redeem you with an outstretched arm." 4. "I will take you to Me for a people."

BACKGROUND:

Passover, also known as Pesach, is a springtime holiday and a pilgrimage festival, celebrating the Exodus from Egypt when Moses led the Jewish people out of slavery. Passover begins in the evening, with the first full moon of Spring, on the 14th of the Jewish month of Nisan and is observed for eight days (7 days in Israel). Thus the first day of Passover falls on the 15th of Nisan. The highlight of Passover is the *Seder* (which means order) and is held on the first and/or second night of Passover. During the service, the Story of Exodus from Egypt is told. The order of the *Seder* is read in a special book called the *Haggadah* (which means narrative). In the *Haggadah*, there is detailed telling of the misery of slavery, the ten plagues, the flight from Egypt, explanations of the Passover symbols, and traditional songs, but there is no mention of Moses. Therefore, Passover is a celebration of the Jewish people, not of Moses. And because the early rabbis were afraid that people would make Moses into a supernatural being, which would confuse the meaning of the Exodus, they left Moses out of the *Haggadah*. During Passover only unleavened bread is eaten to remember the Israelites hasty departure from Egypt when the dough did not have time to rise.

The word Passover comes from the tenth plague when the "Angel of Death" smote the first-born child of every Egyptian but passed over the homes of the Israelites.

The Story of Moses
(A Read-Aloud Story for Passover)

When Moses was a baby, a decree was issued by Pharaoh that every male child born to an Israelite would be killed. Desperate to save their son, Moses' mother, Jochebed, and father, Amram, of the tribe of Levi, placed their child in a basket and set him afloat among the bulrushes of the Nile River. The Egyptian princess, Bitya, found the baby in the basket while she and her handmaidens bathed in the river. The princes called the baby Moses, an Egyptian name that means, "drawn out of the water." Moses' sister, Miriam, had watched what became of her baby brother. Realizing the baby would need milk, Miriam approached the princess and said she knew of a woman (Moses' own mother) who could nurse the baby. The princess agreed and Jochebed was able to nurse her own son until he was two years old. After that Bitya, the princess, raised him as her own son in the palace.

Once when Moses was still a baby, Pharaoh had a great feast for all his ministers. During the feast Pharaoh leaned over towards Moses, and the baby took Pharaoh's crown from his head and put it on his own head, holding it so it would not slip over his eyes. This surprised and alarmed all of Pharaoh's ministers. Pharaoh quickly took his crown back. The chief wizard, Balaam, saw this as a very serious sign that meant Moses would grown up to be king of Egypt rather than Pharaoh and suggested Moses be put to death.

Jethro, the high priest of Midian, then suggested the baby did not know what he was doing and a test should be conducted to see if Moses would always want the crown. Jethro suggested that two pans be placed before Moses, one filled with jewels and one filled with burning charcoal to see which one the baby would touch. If the baby touched the jewels then Pharaoh would know Moses meant to take the crown and that he would always want it. Then the baby would be put to death. But if the baby took the glowing charcoal, it meant that anything bright and shiny attracted him and taking the king's crown was nothing. When the two pans were set before Moses he took a piece of glowing charcoal and brought it to his mouth. The hot charcoal burned his lips and fingers. As a result Moses spoke with a stutter and was unable to speak clearly.

So Moses grew up as a prince in Pharaoh's palace. Moses remembered the home of Jochebed, though he did not know she was his mother, and from time to time he would visit her. On his eighteenth birthday he set out to visit Jochebed. On the way, Moses saw an Egyptian overseer beating an Israelite slave. Moses killed the overseer. After burying the dead body in the sand, Moses went to Jochebed's home. Now that he was eighteen, Jochebed told Moses that he was her son. Now he knew that all the slaves were his own people.

Fearing he would be put to death for killing the Egyptian overseer, Moses fled to the land of Midian in the Sinai desert. He became a shepherd and lived with the priest named Jethro, the very same priest who had saved him as a baby. Moses married Zipproah, Jethro's oldest daughter and she bore him two sons. One day while tending his flock, a little goat ran away from the flock and Moses went after it. The Lord appeard to Moses as a burning bush and told him to go down to Egypt and tell Pharaoh to "Let my people go!" Moses told his father-in-law Jethro, wife Zipporah, and two sons what he had to do. On his way back to Egypt, Moses met his brother Aaron, whom the Lord had sent to speak for him for Moses still stammered and his speech was unclear.

Once in Egypt, Moses and Aaron went directly to the palace to speak to Pharaoh. They pleaded for the Israelites to be set free but Pharaoh refused to listen. So the Lord sent ten plagues to afflict and inconvenience Egypt and Pharaoh. After each plague Moses and Aaron returned to Pharaoh and said, "Let my people go!" Each time Pharaoh would initially agree to set the Israelites free only to change his mind. After the tenth plague when Pharaoh's own son died, Pharaoh allowed the Israelites to go free.

Soon Pharaoh regretted that he had told Moses to leave with his slaves. Now who would finish building his city? So Pharaoh sent his army out after the Israelites. The army caught up with them just as they reached the shores of the Sea of Reeds, the Suez arm of the Red Sea. The Israelites were trapped with the sea before them and Pharaoh's army behind them. Suddenly the Egyptian army was faced with a mass of cloud where they could see nothing ahead of them and thus were forced to stay where they were. The Lord spoke to Moses and told him to "raise your staff over the sea and divide it into two parts." An east wind began to blow, the waters parted and the Israelites were able to walk on dry land to the shore on the other side. As the last of the Israelites entered the Sea of Reeds, the cloud was lifted from in front of the Egyptians. The soldiers reached the water's edge just as the last of the Israelites emerged on the other side. Once again Moses raised his staff and the waters rushed back drowning the soliders in the Sea of Reeds. Miriam, Moses' sister led all the women in a song and dance of joy and celebration.

As the Israelites journeyed in the wilderness they soon used up their food supply they had brought from Egypt. So Moses prayed and the Lord sent food that fell from the sky and became known as _manna_. On Fridays they collected a double protion of _manna_ because on Saturday (Shabbat) they were not allowed to collect food. The Lord decided to give the Torah to the Israelites and Moses spent forty days on top of Mount Sinai to receive it and learn it. When Moses returned from Mount Sinai, Moses noticed that the Israelites did not know yet how to be free and so they went back to their slavish ways. And so the Israelites wandered through the wilderness for forty years so the older generation from Egypt died out. Meanwhile Moses taught the youngsters who were born in the wilderness how to live by the Torah. As this new, free generation grew to adulthood, they were ready and eager to enter the land of Canaan. However, the Lord told Moses that his time had come and he would not be entering the land of Canaan so the people entered the Promise Land after being blessed by Moses.

NOTE: This story of Moses may contain more information than your students need. You may adjust this story to fit the needs of your students.

Game: Frog Math Game
(Matching Sets, Counting)

A GAME FOR PASSOVER

**Before you begin, decide what range of numbers you want to work on and create the game to fit that range.

MATERIALS:
Frog pattern*(p. 111)   Lily pad pattern*(p. 111)   Bug patterns*(p. 110)
File folder   Pencil pouch or envelope
See APPLE NUMBER MATCH GAME for Dot Pattern Suggestion (p.38)

INSTRUCTIONS:
1. Copy the appropriate number of frogs and lily pads onto green paper.

2. Cut out and glue the lily pads to the inside of the file folder.

3. Assign each frog a number and write that numeral in black on the frog. Cut out the frogs.

4. In sequential order place the proper number of one type of bug per lily pad. Arrange the bugs on the lily pads like the dot pattern suggestion and glue down. (For example: 3 caterpillars, 4 spiders, 5 moths, 6 flies, 7 beetles, 8 bees, 9 ladybugs, or butterflies). Note: Store bought "bug" stickers can be used instead of copying the ones provided.

5. Design a dot self-check pattern on the back of the frogs to look like the bug pattern on the lily pad the frog corresponds to.

6. Design a cover and glue the directions to the back.

7. Laminate the frogs and file folder.

8. Attach a pencil pouch or envelope to the back of the folder and store the frogs inside.

DIRECTIONS TO PLAY FROG MATH GAME
(ONE PLAYER)

1. Remove the frogs from the pouch or envelope.

2. The player takes a frog and places it on the lily pad with the corresponding number of bugs.

3. The player can check their own work by turning the frog over to see if the dot pattern matches the bug pattern on the lily pad.

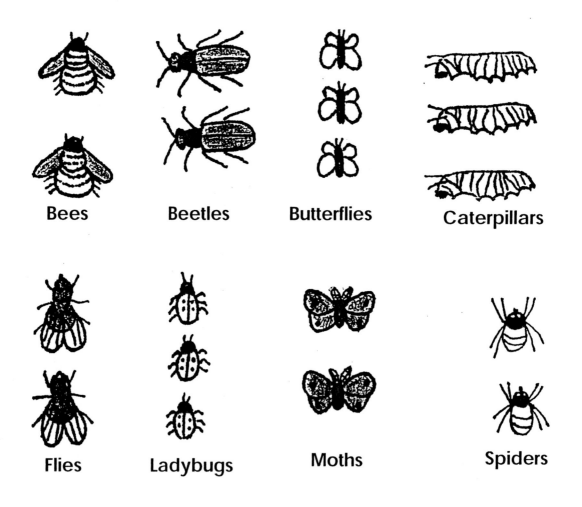

Bees	**Beetles**	**Butterflies**	**Caterpillars**
Flies	**Ladybugs**	**Moths**	**Spiders**

Frog Math Game Lily Pad and Frog Pattern

Game: Frogs on Pharaoh
*(Matching Letters to Letters or Words to Words,
Naming Objects in English and Hebrew)*

A GAME FOR PASSOVER

MATERIALS:
Large file folder   Picture of Pharaoh* (pp. 114. 115)
14 Passover pictures*(pp. 119, 120)   Pencil pouch or envelope
Frog Patterns* (14 with Hebrew letters, 7 blank to add English letters) (pp. 116-118)

INSTRUCTIONS:
1. Copy or draw the top half and bottom half of Pharaoh to fit inside the file folder. Use the fold of the folder to line up the edges of the two halves. If necessary, stretch the middle of the blanket to make the bed longer.

2. Copy and color the 14 Passover pictures. English and Hebrew have been provided with each picture. Cut out each picture leaving the words with each picture. Decide if the game is to stress beginning sounds in English or Hebrew.

3. Make a total of 14 blank frogs for English letters. If using Hebrew, copy the two pages of frogs with the Hebrew letters. Color and cut out the frogs.

4. For English sounds, use a black marker and write the following letters on the frogs: A, B, B, C, E, F, M, O, P, Q, S, S, T, W. (Note: There are two pictures beginning with the letters 'B' and 'S.')

5. Arrange the Passover pictures on the blanket and glue down. The pictures can be used with English only, Hebrew only or both, Teacher's choice.

6. Design a cover for the file folder and glue the directions to the back.

7. Laminate the frogs and file folder.

8. Store the frogs in a pencil pouch or envelope attached to the back of the folder.

DIRECTIONS TO PLAY FROGS ON PHARAOH
(ONE PLAYER)

1. Remove the frogs from the pencil pouch or envelope.

2. The player places the correct letter (frog) on top of the corresponding picture. The player could name each picture out loud.

3. When complete, Pharaoh will have his bed covered with frogs.

EXAMPLE:

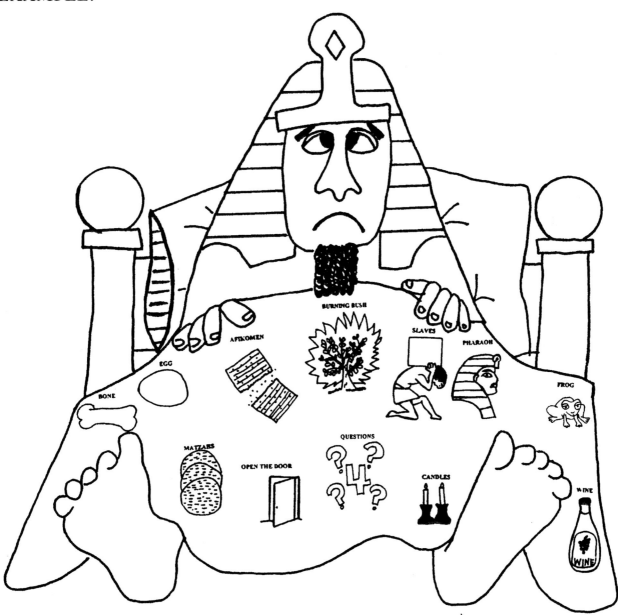

Top Half of Pharaoh

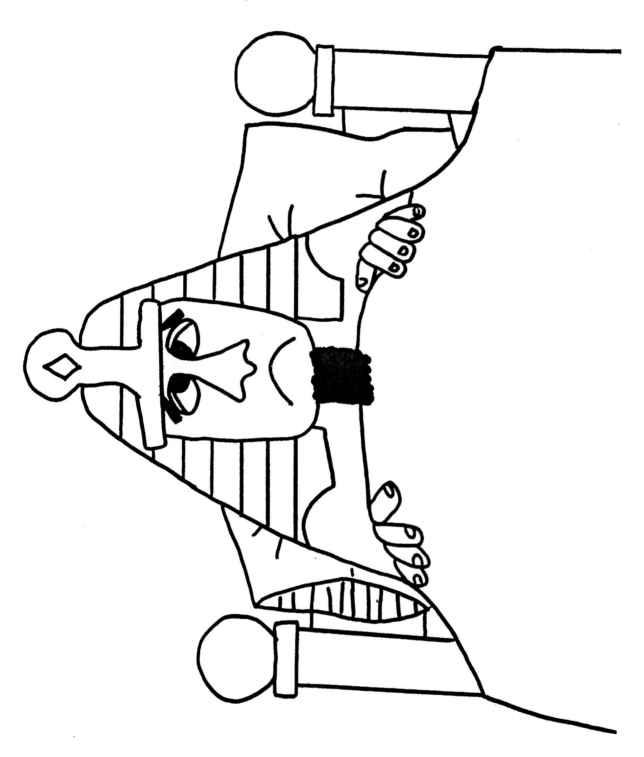

Bottom Half of Pharaoh

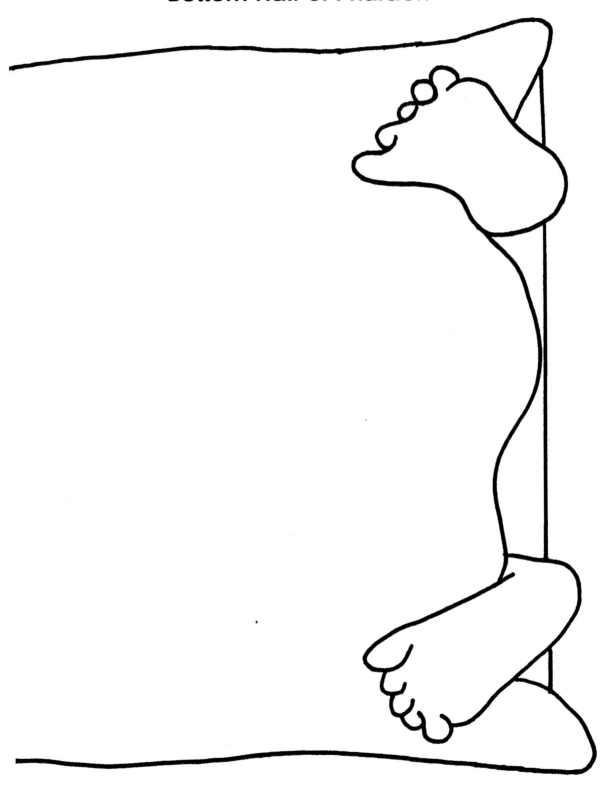

Blank Frog Patterns (for English letters)

Hebrew Frog Patterns

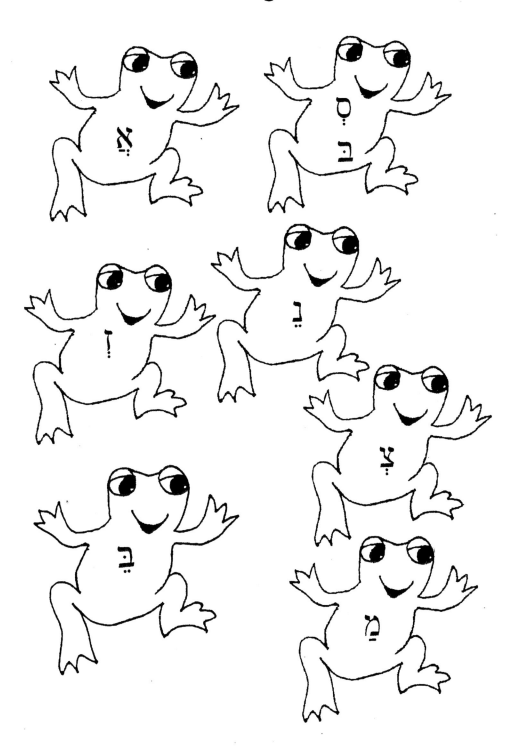

Hebrew Frog Patterns

Frogs on Pharaoh Passover Pictures

Afikomen

אֲפִיקוֹמֶן

af-fee-ko-<u>man</u>

Burning Bush

סְנֶה בּוֹעֵר

<u>sne</u> bo-<u>er</u>
(bush burn)

Bone

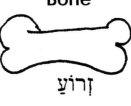

זְרוֹעַ

<u>zro</u>-a

Candles

נֵרוֹת

ne-<u>rot</u>

Egg

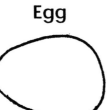

בֵּיצָה

bei-<u>tsa</u>

Frog

צְפַרְדֵעַ

tsfar-<u>de</u>-ah

Matzahs

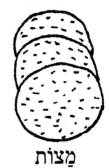

מַצּוֹת

ma-<u>tsot</u>

Frogs on Pharaoh Passover Pictures

Open the Door

לִפְתּוֹחַ אֶת הַדֶּלֶת

lif-<u>to</u>-ach <u>et</u> ha-<u>de</u>-let

Pharaoh

פַּרְעֹה

par-o

Questions

קוּשְׁיוֹת

koo-shi-<u>yot</u>

Seder Plate

קְעָרָה

keh-ah-<u>rah</u>

(plate)

Slaves

עֲבָדִים

ah-va-<u>dim</u>

Tears

דְּמָעוֹת

dma-<u>ot</u>

Wine

יַיִן

<u>ya</u>-yin

Game: Seder Plate
(1 to 1 Correspondence)

A GAME FOR PASSOVER

MATERIALS:
Seder plate pattern*(p. 123)   Large manila envelope

INSTRUCTIONS:
1. Enlarge and copy the Seder plate ten times.

2. Use five plates to be the game board. Color the background of these plates its own color.

3. Color the symbols of all plates to be as realistic as possible.

4. Cut apart the individual circles from the remaining five plates.

5. Design a cover for the manila envelope and glue the directions to the back.

6. Laminate the five plates, 25 symbols and envelope.

7. Store the game pieces in the envelope.

DIRECTIONS TO PLAY SEDER PLATE GAME
(1-5 PLAYERS)

1. Players select their own Seder plate.

2. Keep the 25 symbols inside the envelope.

3. Decide who will go first. The first player reaches into the envelope, pulls out one symbol, and places it on their plate.

4. The second player goes and play continues to all players.

5. If a player selects a symbol that is already on their plate, the symbol is returned to the envelope and play continues to the next player.

6. When a player has all five symbols on their plate, they say, "HAPPY PASSOVER!" (or "פֶּסַח שָׂמֵחַ" (pe-sach sa-mei-ach) in Hebrew).

Seder Plate Pattern

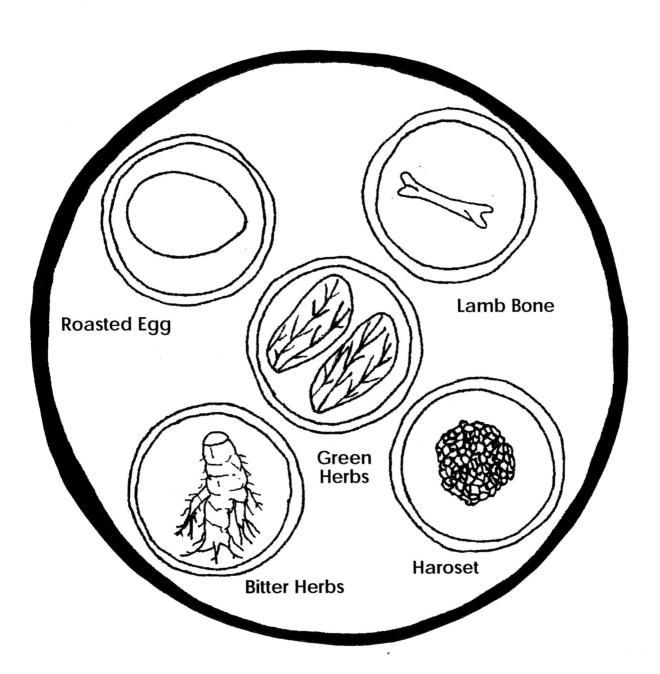

Roasted Egg

Lamb Bone

Green
Herbs

Bitter Herbs

Haroset

Game: Butterfly Wing Match Up
(Visual Discrimination)

A GAME FOR SPRING

MATERIALS:
Butterfly pattern*(p. 126)   Tag board   Large envelope
Multi-colored 3/4" self-adhesive circles (for example: blue, green, red, yellow, white)

INSTRUCTIONS:
1. Copy the butterfly pattern 10 times onto tag board.

2. Decorate the wings by placing 1 or 2 dots of the same color on each wing half.

3. Cut out the butterflies and cut in half.

4. Laminate the wings.

5. Design a cover for the envelope and glue the directions to the back.

6. Store the game pieces inside the envelope.

DIRECTIONS TO PLAY BUTTERFLY WING MATCH UP
(1-2 PLAYERS)

1. Arrange the wings face down on a table.

2. Decide who will go first. The first player turns over two wings.

3. If the wings match, the player keeps the wings to form a butterfly.

4. If the wings do not match, the wings are returned to the table and the next player goes.

5. The game continues until all the matching wing pairs have been selected.

Butterfly Wing Match Up Pattern

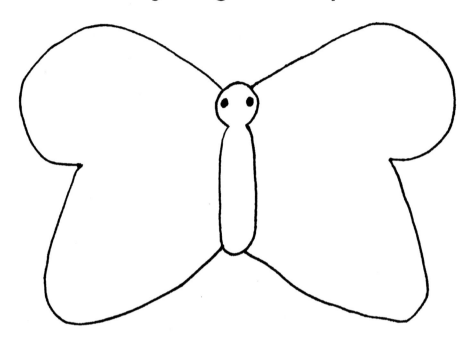

EXAMPLE:

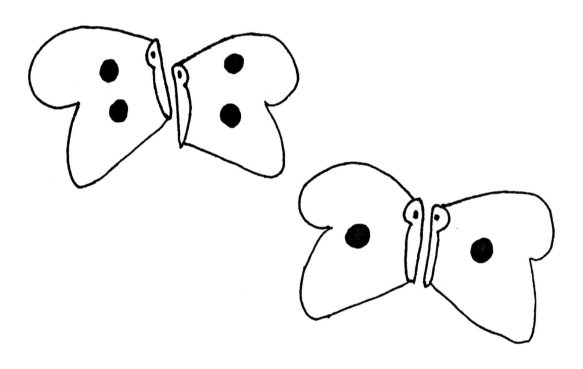

Game: Build a Pyramid
(Matching and Recognizing Colors:
Blue, Green, Orange, Purple, Red, and Yellow in English and Hebrew)

A GAME FOR PASSOVER

MATERIALS:
Four Pyramid patterns* (1 set in Hebrew, 1 set in English) (pp. 129-132)
Tag board   Small cloth pouch or bag
Optional: 1" colored cubes (Six colors: blue, green, orange, purple, red, yellow; four of each)

INSTRUCTIONS:
1. Copy either the four Hebrew or the four English Pyramid patterns two times onto tag board. Color all the squares ("bricks") per color. For the Hebrew Pyramids, use the color chart below to color each square correctly.

2. Color the boarders of four Pyramids, four neutral colors (like brown, tan, black, or gray). Use these four Pyramids as the gameboards. Cut out these four Pyramids into a triangle shape.

3. Cut apart the squares on the remaining four Pyramids to be the "bricks".

4. Laminate the four Pyramid gameboards and all the "bricks."

5. Store the game in a cloth pouch or bag. Enclose the directions.

Note: If colored cubes are used as "bricks," only make one set of the Pyramid patterns. Color the squares ("bricks") per color. Color the borders four neutral colors and cut out. Laminate the four Pyramids. Store the game in a small cloth pouch or bag. Enclose the directions.

DIRECTIONS TO PLAY BUILD A PYRAMID GAME
(1-4 PLAYERS)

1. Players select their own Pyramid. Leave the "bricks" inside the cloth pouch or bag.

2. Decide who will go first. The first player reaches inside the cloth pouch or bag without looking and selects one "brick."

3. The player places the "brick" on their Pyramid game board by matching the colors, and thus begins building the Pyramid.

4. The next player takes a turn reaching in the cloth pouch or bag.

5. If a "brick" is picked that is already on their Pyramid game board, the "brick" is returned to the cloth pouch or bag and the player's turn ends.

6. Play continues until all the "bricks" have been used and the Pyramids are built.

COLOR CHART

Blue	ka-<u>chol</u>	כָּחוֹל
Green	ya-<u>rok</u>	יָרוֹק
Orange	ka-<u>tom</u>	כָּתוֹם
Purple	sa-<u>gol</u>	סָגוֹל
Red	a-<u>dom</u>	אָדוֹם
Yellow	tsa-<u>hov</u>	צָהוֹב

English Pyramid Patterns

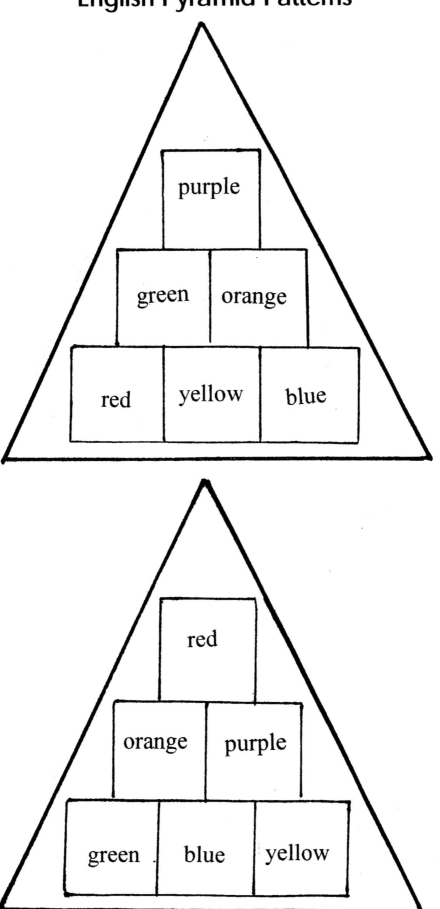

English Pyramid Patterns

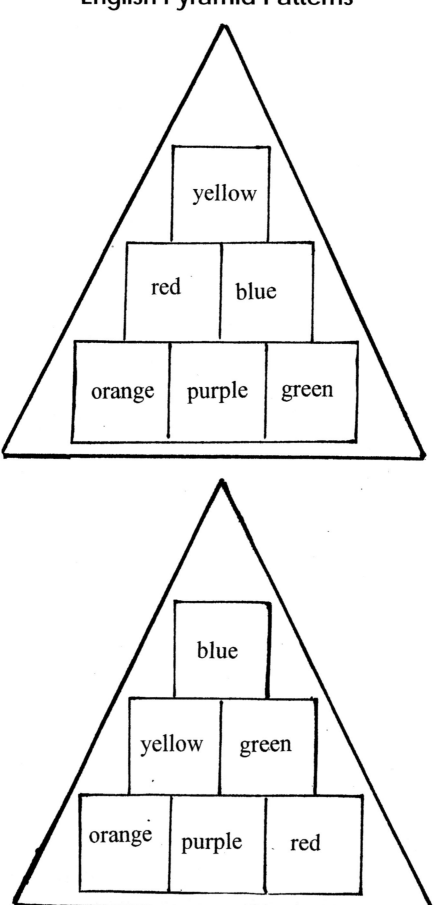

Hebrew Pyramid Patterns

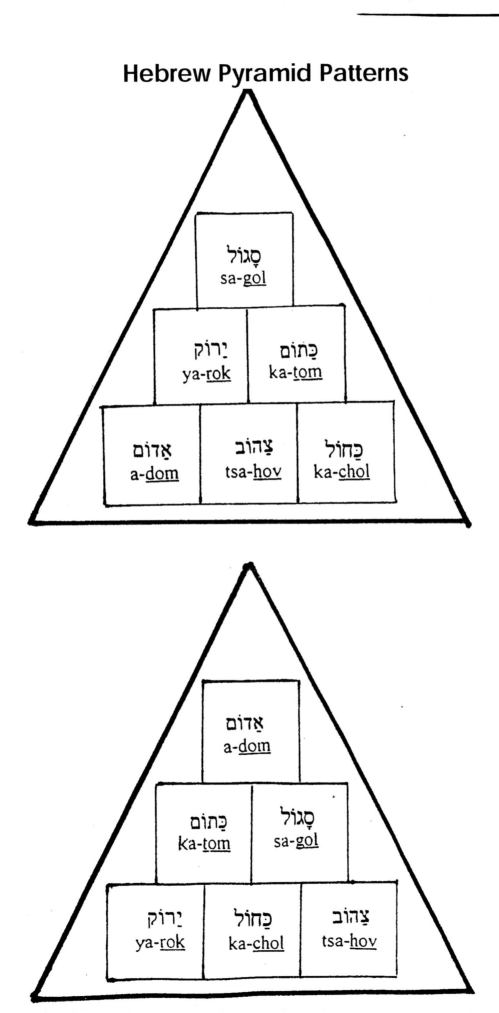

Hebrew Pyramid Patterns

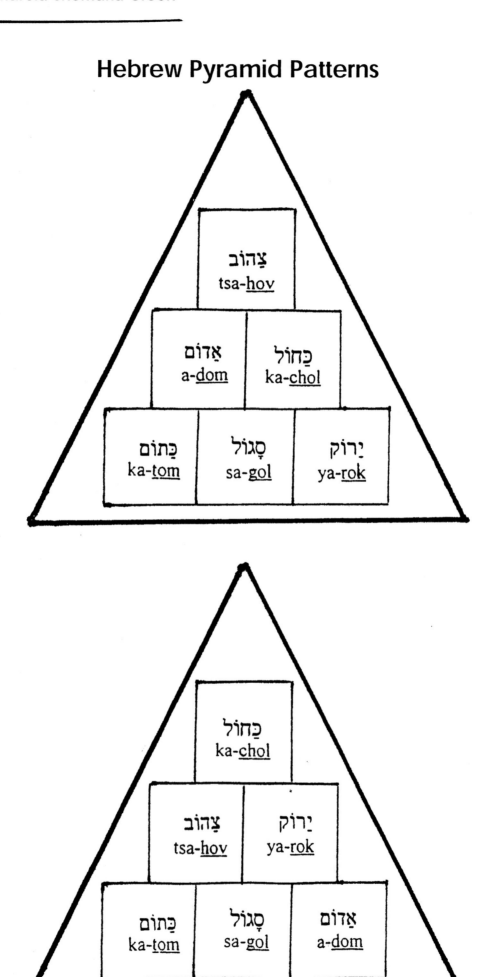

ROSH
CHODESH
AND
CREATION

Background Information for Rosh Chodesh

BACKGROUND:

Rosh Chodesh is a calendar holiday. The Jewish calendar is based on the phases of the moon. Rosh Chodesh (Head of the Month) is the Jewish celebration of the new moon and thus the beginning of a new Hebrew month. A solar year of 12 months is 365 days long and a moon year of 12 months is 354 days long. In order to be sure that the Jewish Holidays occur at their proper season in the year a "leap month", or extra month is added 7 times every nineteen years. The leap years in this 19-year period fall during the third, sixth, eighth, eleventh, fourteenth, seventeenth, and nineteenth years. When it is a leap year, an extra month is added after the Hebrew month of Adar and is called "Adar Sheni", or Adar the second. In this way, the Jewish people have successfully synchronized the lunar calendar with the solar cycle.

"Night Sky, Night Sky What Do You See?"
(Phases of the Moon, Sequencing)

A ROSH CHODESH RHYME

MATERIALS:
9 Pages to "Night Sky, Night Sky, What Do You See?"

INSTRUCTIONS:
1. Copy the 9 pages to "Night Sky, Night Sky, What Do You See?"

2. Laminate the pages and bind the pages into a "book" form.

Night Sky, Night Sky,

What Do You See?

by Marcia Shemaria Green

Night sky, night sky what do you see?
I see a (waxing) crescent moon coming to be.

Night sky, night sky what do you see?
I see a half moon (first quarter) as even as can be.

Night sky, night sky what do you see?
I see a three-quarter (waxing Gibbous) moon glowing at me.

Night sky, night sky what do you see?
I see a big, bright full moon shining at me.

Night sky, night sky what do you see?
I see a three-quarter (waning Gibbous) moon looking at me.

Night sky, night sky what do you see
I see a last quarter moon as even as can be.

Night sky, night sky what do you see?
I see a (waning) crescent moon as small as can be.

Night sky, night sky what do you see?
I see no moon (New Moon) looking at me.

Game: Space Game
(Counting 1-6 or 6-1, Sequencing)

A GAME FOR THE STORY OF CREATION

MATERIALS:

Earth pattern*(p. 147)   Moon pattern*(p. 147)   Star pattern*(p. 147)
1 Die   File folder   Pencil pouch
4 "Spaceship" movers (different colored marker tops or toothpaste tops)

INSTRUCTIONS:

1. Copy the Earth and Moon patterns. Color and cut out the Earth and Moon.

2. Inside the file folder, glue the Earth in the upper left corner and the Moon in the lower right corner.

3. Use the pattern of the Stars as a stencil. By tracing around a Star pattern, design a snake-like path from the Earth to the Moon using as many stars as necessary. Outline the Stars in a varying color pattern.

4. Design a cover and glue the directions to the back of the file folder.

5. Laminate the file folder. Attach the pencil pouch to the back of the file folder to hold the die and movers.

DIRECTIONS TO PLAY THE SPACE GAME
(2-4 PLAYERS)

1. Each player selects a "spaceship" (mover) and places it on the Earth.

2. Decide who will go first. The first player rolls the die and moves the appropriate number of Stars toward the Moon.

3. The second player goes. Play continues until all the "space ships" land on the moon.

VARIATION: Start on the Moon and with each roll of the die count backwards to reach the Earth. (Example: A five is rolled on the die. The player moves and counts out loud five, four, three, two, one.)

Space Game Patterns

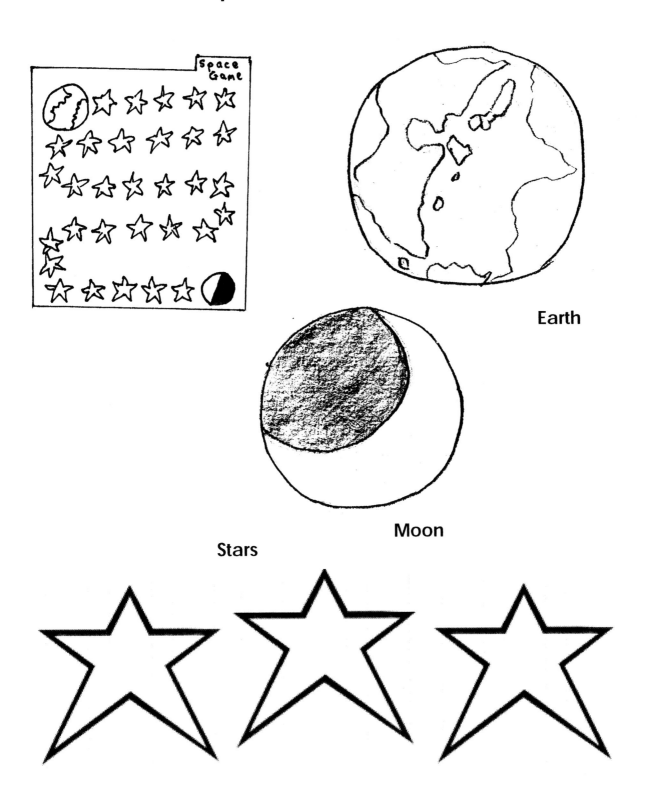

Earth

Moon

Stars

A Story of Creation
(A Read-Aloud Story)

In the beginning, there was a watery vastness without life or light there was only darkness. Only the spirit of God moved across the darkness.

Then God said, "Let there be light." And there was light. God called the light "Day" and the darkness he called "Night." And there was evening and morning on the first day.

On the second day, God divided the vastness above and below. He called the upper part "Heaven." And there was evening and morning on the second day.

On the third day, God gathered the waters below into one area and allowed the dry land to appear. God called the dry land "Earth" and the gathered waters He called "Seas." And God said let the Earth spout vegetation, seed-bearing plants, and fruit trees of every kind. And God saw that this was good. And there was evening and morning on the third day.

On the fourth day, God made two great lights, the greater light to dominate the day (the Sun) and the lesser light to dominate the night and the stars (the Moon). And God saw that this was good. And there was evening and morning on the fourth day.

On the fifth day, God created fish of every kind to live in the waters and winged birds of every kind. And God saw that this was good. Then God blessed them, saying, "Be fertile and increase, fill the waters in the seas, and let the birds increase on the Earth." And there was evening and morning on the fifth day.

On the sixth day, God said, "Let the Earth bring forth every kind of living creature: cattle, creeping things, and wild beasts of every kind." And God saw that this was good. Then God created Man to rule over every creature that swims the waters, flies in the sky, and roamed or creeps on the land. God called the Man, "Adam." But God did not want Adam to be alone so he created Woman. He called her "Eve." God blessed them and said to them, "Be fertile and increase, fill the Earth and master it; and rule the fish, the birds, and all the living things that creep on the Earth." And God found this was good. And there was evening and morning on the sixth day.

On the seventh day, God finished the work that He had been doing and he rested. And God blessed the seventh day and declared it holy.

ABOUT THE AUTHOR

Marcia Shemaria Green has been a Preschool teacher at the Weinstein School in Atlanta, Ga since 1986 and holds a degree in Early Childhood Education from the University of Georgia. In May of 1998, Marcia was the first recipient from her school to receive a Certificate of Appreciation for "Dedication and Excellence in Teaching."

Printed in the United States
44957LVS00007B/75-84

9 780893 343446